21 MARCH '79

FOR CAROLYN + PAUL
WHOM I RESPECT AND
TRUST—

Ed Bryant

# Will It Matter What I Was?

# Will It Matter What I Was?

*Eve [to Cain] You despise your father; but when he dies the world will be the richer because he lived. When you die, men will say, 'He was a great warrior; but it would have been better for the world if he had never been born.' And of Lua they will say nothing; but when they think of her they will spit.*

George Bernard Shaw, *Back to Methuselah*

The tall man spoke my name. Said I was
not too bad a guy. He'd known me
for some while, but hadn't had a chance
to get the story of my life. I'd
come from someplace else; it was his view
I never really belonged here anyway.
Sam Lane, his chair eased back against the wall,
put in that I was smart, and never at a loss
for words—that if they seemed a foreign language
it was just my way. He'd tried to think
of stuff I'd said, but like a paycheck cashed
and spent, it always got away real quick.
Oh, I remember him, some kid made out.
That winter when the big snow came his car
slid off and me and Tom got called upon
to push. He gave us each a five—way too
much we thought, but took it anyway.
And Mister George, who always had a word
to say, allowed as how I never tried
to get along with local folks, but stayed
so busy that I plumb wore out before
my time—a shame, he said. Then round
the circle of that ended council on
my worth, they barely knowing shook their heads.
And saying nothing more they thought to go
as silence muttered to the wind outside.

# Will It Matter What I Was?

## EDWARD C. BRIGGS

Broadman Press, Nashville, Tennessee

4252–61
ISBN: 0–8054–5261–3

Scripture quotations are from the Revised Standard Version unless otherwise
indicated. © Division of Christian Education of the National Council of Churches
of Christ in the United States of America, 1946, 1952.

Dewey Decimal Classification: 252
Subject heading: SERMONS

Library of Congress Catalog Card Number: 77–87250
*Printed in the United States of America*

# Foreword

Ed Briggs's WILL IT MATTER WHAT I WAS? is prime stuff. Here is basic theology without the clumsy jargon which often weighs theology down. Here is immediate help for those of us who find the Christian way very difficult and who hoot at the propaganda which says that the Christian pilgrimage is all happiness and bliss. Here is help for the thoughtful who live on the rough edges of life and still wonder when their deliverance will come.

Ed Briggs brings to this book a well-furnished mind, a heart enlarged by suffering, and a skillful pen. He is a compelling communicator of the gospel.

These sermons center on human problems. But, unlike much psychological preaching, they are much more than an analysis of our human dilemma. Ed Briggs knows what to do with human dilemmas. He takes them straight to God. A bishop in the Episcopal Church, a student of Harry Emerson Fosdick, once corrected me when I insisted that Fosdick's sermons always centered on a specific human problem. "Yes," he said, "but in his lectures on preaching Fosdick always said, 'state the human problem but don't let more than sixty seconds pass until you get into the Scriptures.'" These sermons do that.

Here we have sermons which also acknowledge that God is the great beginning point. He talks about "A Divine Perspective on the Human Situation." He has what Carlyle Marney calls "the cheeky imperiousness of the preacher." He dares to ask, Who is this God who "sits in the heavens"? What does he do? What can we know of him? What does he think of us? He acknowledges that what God knows about us is infinitely more important than what we know about God. Nevertheless he believes that what we know about God is important. The God of the Bible is a God who "speaks; he comes; he goes; he returns. He sees and walks and visits and rests."

Other times we see him as dark and forbidding. He judges and forbids and is angry and condemns. He hates, avenges, overthrows, destroys.

"But then at other times we see him as our joy and hope. He saves and redeems and preserves and shows mercy. He blesses and promises. He provides for us; he gives refuge; he wipes away our tears; he makes us kings and priests." He is also a God who laughs and mocks. God laughs as we play our little games of finding fault in others to justify ourselves. As if the plan of salvation were to rid ourselves of sin by finding it in other people.

Ed Briggs writes incisively of the value of creative insecurity. He puts down the world's concept of strength which is epitomized in the "jugular instinct."

He talks about the strength of a bank president who enjoys delivering newspapers. He also speaks about a Ph.D. who is a garbage collector in the summertime. A woman stood watching from the back porch as he emptied her garbage into his sack. As he shouldered it to leave, she asked, "Do you think you'll ever amount to anything?" The Ph.D. walked away laughing.

This book will bring help to all who read it.

CHARLES A. TRENTHAM
*First Baptist Church*
*Washington, D. C.*

# Contents

Part IV Integrity as an Inner Honesty

Part V Integrity as Personal Wholeness

# Part I

## Perspectives on Integrity

Dear Father (heavenly):

I'm confused. People keep telling me that you're up there looking at me—seeing what I do, and even knowing what I think.

That seems reasonable when I go to church, what with all those people so serious and reverent. You seem near then.

But on other days, I really wonder whether it matters to you if I'm good or bad, rich or poor, dead or alive.

I wish I could know, because it's an awful lot of trouble to keep those rules they say you've given us. I mean—if I knew it didn't matter to you, life would be much simpler all the way around.

Is there any kind of help you could give me with this?

# 1

## Will It Matter What I Was?

*Will it matter what I was? The dead are gone, aren't they? Just walk around and look—a few flowers in a vase, a few old pictures fading in a drawer, an estate for some heirs to squabble over, a name and some dates on a polished marble headstone. "Stanley L. Williams: born 1837, died 1902." "John R. Lopez, Virgil C. Painter, Max Rosenberg"—they lived; they died. They came; they went away. They were here; now they're gone. Did it matter who they were, or what they were, or that they were at all?*

*Will it matter what I was? It seems not to matter when I'm tired and spent and all used up; when I'm misunderstood; when I'm the only one who cares. It seems not to matter when the drumbeat I'm trying to keep time to is almost drowned out by the cacophony of all those others. It seems not to matter when the leader I put my trust in has just forsaken the best of my expectations for him. It seems not to matter when wickedness and evil bring prosperity and reward, and goodness only brings trouble.*

*"Good guys finish last . . . Every man has his price . . . God helps those who help themselves . . . Do unto others before they do you in . . . Don't be a fool; look out for Number One." This is what they say; and if this be wisdom, why am I beating my head against a wall?*

*Why should I be moral instead of immoral, informed instead of ignorant, or truthful instead of lying? Whose authority tells me to be brave instead of cowardly, or generous instead of stingy? What if I'm peaceful, not violent, or neat, not sloppy; what does it matter?*

*Where do I get this uneasy feeling that someone's looking over my shoulder and watching my work? Why does an unrelenting moral struggle have to go on for so long after I've declared my freedom and independence?*

*Please . . . please, excuse me from the course. I'll just take an F, and go on my way. It doesn't matter to me; I just want out. I don't want these questions; I don't want these assignments; I don't want this feeling of pressure; and I don't want to take that final examination. Please . . . isn't there something to be done in a case like mine?* [1]

It may be well hidden away, but I suspect there's some of that feeling in almost all of us—that wondering if achievement and integrity is really worth it. The writer of Ecclesiastes expressed this long ago, as he asked: *What has a man from all the toil and strain with which he toils beneath the sun?* (Eccl. 2:22). The question is one of those basic ones we keep putting aside in order to finish the day's work. But it is one that needs an answer, if the work is to be rewarding. And it's one we ought not put off so long that we come upon it with most of our years behind us, and very few left ahead. That thought is in Ecclesiastes, too. It says: "Remember also your Creator in the days of your youth, before the evil days come, and the years draw nigh, when you will say, 'I have no pleasure in them' " (12:1).

Are you aware that our modern world isn't exactly kind or friendly to idealists? When everyone else is taking shortcuts, it's pretty hard for the person who insists on going by the rules. No one likes a tattletale, but how can we avoid some responsibility for dealing with the wrongdoing which abounds? And in a competitive world it's not easy to fall behind, just because you were unwilling to adopt the tactics of the other side. So what I'm getting at is an assurance that it matters what we are, because without it our idealism (and thus our religion) will be either a failure or a frustration.

14

Will it matter what I was? *It matters—before the cross it matters*. For on that hill called Golgotha, God showed us how much some things matter.

*The cross shows God's unwillingness to look upon man's sin as something which doesn't matter*. Paul expressed it this way: "While we were yet sinners, Christ died for us" (Rom. 5:8).

Someone died? For us? What strange talk is that? We didn't ask for any such thing, and we don't prefer to think about that point of theology. Just give us a Christ with words to listen to and an example to follow. Who needs this "dying for our sins"? Just give us Jesus, the superintellectual; or Jesus, the outstanding young man; or Jesus, the founder and organizer of our religion. That atonement stuff is a little too personal; don't you see? To justify that bloody cross as an act of God's love, you have to face the seriousness and offense of our sin. Apart from that consideration, God seems to be rather overreacting.

The cross also shows us this—*It shows God's estimate of how much one solitary life can matter*. Have you ever noticed the hint of that in John 3:16? "God so loved the world that he gave his only Son, that whoever believes in him should not perish but have eternal life." On one hand God looked at our vast world and all its sin; on the other hand he considered his only Son. And God decided that the one could make a difference in the other. And so we can sing, in the anthem by Sir John Goss: "O Saviour of the world, who by Thy Cross and precious Blood hast redeemed us; Save us and help us, we humbly beseech Thee, O Lord, O Saviour of the world!" [2]

So the cross is a demonstration of the difference one life can make. And although I certainly recognize the uniqueness of that event—none of us can hope to matter *that* much—I still carry away a feeling that because *his* life mattered *ours* can also. This surely is why he challenged his followers: "If any man would come after me, let him . . . take up *his* cross, and follow me" (Matt. 16:24). Why would he ask us to do that if his was the only

15

cross that mattered—if the heavenly voice doesn't also speak to more ordinary folk and say: "You are one of my many beloved sons, in whom I am well pleased"?

In other words, the cross shows the importance God attaches to the quality of our human existence. He has here given us an estimate of our worth. This is how much it's worth to God to recover that *imageo deo* we started out with, that got tarnished on the way. Jesus said that his coming was to offer us "life," and "that more abundantly" (John 10:10, KJV). And God is a fool if it cannot be said that man is worth that price, that his life matters that much.

Will it matter what I was? *I say it matters—in the heart of man it matters.* Everybody wants to be somebody—important to someone, needed for something. Sure, my life matters to God in heaven, but there's an inner thing as well. It matters to *me*. Call it self-respect; call it ego-need; call it a survival-wish; call it anything you like; it's still there, and you know it.

Materialism is bankrupt. Something inside won't let us believe that it matters as much what we *have* as what we *are*. That's how the SLA was able to make a convert out of Patricia Hearst. They had this edge—that a person's need to matter is greater than his need to inherit money. They found a poor rich girl who couldn't imagine how it was going to matter who she was, and they gave her the chance to do it big.

In fact, you'd better not tell anyone who ever made much of a difference to the world that his life doesn't matter. You couldn't have said that to Dwight Eisenhower or Harry Truman or Martin Luther King or Casey Stengel. Don't try to tell George Wallace that. It'd sound silly to say that to Gary Player or Billy Graham or Bella Abzug or Dr. Christian Barnard. What do all those people have in common? Nothing, really, except that each of them, in his own way, believes that it will matter what he was. And it will.

Imagine finding distressed Nicodemus on his way to see Jesus by night, and saying to him: "Nick, aren't you taking your religion a little too seriously?" Imagine finding the prodigal son on the way back home to his father, and saying to him: "Now boy, don't you think you're a little too upset about this?" Imagine catching Martin Luther on his way to the Wittenberg church door, and asking him if he really believed this soon-to-be-nailed-up document would make any difference!

Those aren't just special people. They are all of us who feel the need for a life which matters. And the need shows when an auto assembly worker chalks his initials on the inside of a car door, or a concrete finisher leaves his name and a date engraved in a new sidewalk. It shows when someone sets out to break a record and get his name in the book. It shows when a man buys more prestige in a car than he can really afford. It shows when a woman keeps her phone line hot for two solid weeks, just outmaneuvering her rival for the club presidency.

*Here, look at me. It matters who I am! You're going to remember me. I was really somebody!*

But our problem is that wealth and fame alone won't do it. They run dry. They lose their power to satisfy our need. You see, we've landed right in the middle of a moral universe, and we can't set the rules for ourselves. There's an "oughtness" down inside, which relates to God and the way he made us. And if we want our success to be enduring, we must reckon with that.

Will it matter what I was? *I say again, it matters—for the future it matters.* Thomas Carlyle said: "The poorest day that passes over us is the conflux of two Eternities; it is made up of currents that issue from the remotest Past and flow onwards into the remotest Future." [3] And that slice of time we're given—bounded at one end by the date of our birth, and on the other by the date of our death—that time may matter significantly to the world we leave behind us. What we are will matter to the future, just as the persons who made the past have mattered so much to us. It's like the book of Hebrews says of Abel; "Through his faith he is still speaking" (11:4).

And if our lives matter for the world we leave behind us, they also matter for whatever future lies before us. How can this be? Listen: "I was hungry and you gave me food, I was thirsty and you gave me drink, I was a stranger and you welcomed me, I was naked and you clothed me, I was sick and you visited me, I was in prison and you came to me" (Matt. 25:35–36). *What do you mean, Lord. When did we see you in need and do all these things?* (Matt. 25:37–39). The king will answer: "As you did it to one of the least of these my brethren, you did it to me . . . . Come, O blessed of my Father, inherit the kingdom prepared for you from the foundation of the world" (Matt. 25:40,34).

There's another side to that, as you well know. We have a choice as to what kind of persons we become. We don't have to care about the hungry. We don't have to do anything for the stranger. We don't have to think about those in prison if we don't want to. But listen to this: "As you did it not to one of the least of these, you did it not to me" (Matt. 25:45). That's the King talking. To some he says "Come, ye blessed," and to others he says, "Depart from me."

And as we reflect upon these lives of ours—lives which will form the basis for that judgment—surely no one can believe that it will not matter what he was.

# 2

# God Laughs

Who is this God who "sits in the heavens"? (Ps. 2:4). What does he do? What can we know of him? What does he think of us?

All we can really know of God is what he has chosen to reveal. You see, the Tower of Babel didn't work; we can't invade his territory. What we have are glimpses, glimpses of who he is and what he does.

Sometimes we see him as much like us. He speaks; he comes; he goes; he returns. He sees and walks and visits and rests.

Other times we see him as dark and forbidding. He judges and forbids and is angry and condemns. He hates, avenges, over-throws, destroys.

But then at other times we see him as our joy and hope. He saves and redeems and preserves and shows mercy. He blesses and promises. He provides for us; he gives us refuge; he wipes away our tears; he makes us kings and priests.

Always in these glimpses we see his power and glory. He creates; he sends the rain; he plants a garden. He commands and reigns and does wonders. He searches men's hearts; he smites his enemies; he scatters the wicked. Sometimes he hides himself; other times he shows his Glory.[4]

But of all the verbs of God's action, perhaps the strangest, the most sobering, and the most devastating is this—*He laughs*. We find it in the second Psalm. There the nations are taking counsel; the kings are exalting themselves; the vanity of men is craving self-glory. And then it says: *He who sits in the heavens laughs* (Ps.

2:1–4).

I think there's a matter of perspective here which may have great value for us: we being so serious about our business, and God laughing; we acting like we have all the answers, and God laughing; we living as if we're in control of things, and God, who made us, looking down from heaven and laughing. What I think we may gain is a kind of perspective for integrity. From God's laughter we may learn to value things he values, and see men as he sees them, and even to look at ourselves as he looks at us.

What do you do with a God who laughs? Isn't he supposed to listen and be serious when we speak with him? Shouldn't he be impressed when we tell of our achievements? Isn't it a bit undignified to think of the Almighty laughing?

Laughter is for old friends remembering the mischief they used to get into. Laughter is for people hearing bad jokes after they've been drinking too much. Laughter is the scorn of youth, who laugh at their elders; or elders, who laugh at their youth. Laughter is for the guy who puts his foot in his mouth, and giggling, sixth-grade girls discussing the facts of life. Bars and markets and roadways and street corners—those are the places where laughing goes on. But heaven? God laughing? Who can imagine that?

Let's remember that when God's Son was here in the flesh, one of the ways some people responded to him was to laugh. It happened in Capernaum when he told a crowd of paid mourners that a little child wasn't dead, only sleeping. "They laughed at him," it says. (See Matt. 9:24.) One version (KJV) says, "They laughed him to scorn." Three of the four Gospels tell us that story, and each one records the laughing.

What must God in heaven think when he sends his Son and men laugh? How must he feel when he offers love and help, and men laugh? What can be said when men encounter one who gave his very life's blood for their sakes, and they laugh him to scorn?

In the context of that rejection, you can almost understand a

20

passage like one in Proverbs which says: *Because I have called and you refused to listen, have stretched out my hand and no one has heeded, and you have ignored all my counsel and would have none of my reproof,* I also will laugh at your calamity; *I will mock when panic strikes you, when panic strikes you like a storm, and your calamity comes like a whirlwind, when distress and anguish come upon you.* (Prov. 1:24–27). Strong words like those sound out of character for God. God mustn't talk like that! He's the Great Approver, bound to bless us in whatever we do, no matter how bad it is. Sure, we all sin, but he mustn't take it personally. Here he is, laughing at the fall of the wicked. He's acting like us!

When a contractor who's been making crooked deals to cheat his clients gets caught, and his facade of respectability comes tumbling down—do you mean God laughs?

When a pleasure-seeker, who laughed at morality while indulging every lust, finds there's nothing left but a great emptiness—do you mean God laughs?

When a national administration, which came into office preaching "have no pity on lawbreakers," is found conspiring to break its own laws and begging for mercy—do you mean God laughs? [5]

Having said this, I think we must add that there are some things God never laughs at: things like hunger and poverty, grief and loneliness, pain and disease, and injustice. But I think the idea of God laughing is something to look into, so let's try listing some of the things he may laugh at.

To begin with, *God laughs at all our claims of goodness.* "There is none righteous, no, not one" (Rom. 3:10, KJV) the Bible says. "All have sinned and fall short of the glory of God" verse 23 says. And when that religious showman stood in the Temple and bragged to God in a prayer—talked about how holy he was, and how he tithed and fasted and wasn't like other people—can't you hear God somewhere laughing? (See Luke 18:9–14.) If I may say so, God was somewhat irreverent on that occasion, laughing at a man's prayer. But I think he had the right. And I'm not at all sure

21

he'd mind if we joined him.

Doesn't God laugh as we play our little games of finding fault in others to justify ourselves? As if the plan of salvation were to rid ourselves of sin by finding it in other people.

*"Did you see what she was wearing? I guess that tells you what kind of person she is!"*

*"Well, you know, that's just the way young people do today. I think it's a disgrace!"*

*"How can anyone come to church and sing in the choir when she has children who act like that?"*

*"I may not go to church a lot, but at least I'm not a hypocrite like those who do."*

On and on we play that game, and God laughs as we do it. Augustine called such pride "the beginning of all sin." And he said: "What is pride, but a perverse desire of height, in forsaking Him to whom the soul ought solely to cleave, as the beginning thereof, to make the self seem the beginning . . . . The soul abandons Him to whom it ought to cleave as its end, and becomes a kind of end in itself." [6]

Bertrand Russell once said that every man would like to be God if that were possible, and some folks find it hard to admit the impossibility! [7]

If God laughs at our claims to goodness, I think *he also laughs at what we call wealth.* He laughs when a man makes a few dollars, enough to buy some acres of "valuable" property—a tiny speck of creation—and then tries to believe that this proves his importance!

I saw it illustrated at a football game in Knoxville once. The man who sat on the aisle seat, a few rows down, was obviously a man of means. His clothes and his bearing, his friends, and the brand of whiskey he sipped—all spoke of it. The man who stood shyly in the aisle, wanting past to get to his seat, was clearly on a different social level. They made him stand there, embarrassed, until at last he went all the way around the entire crowded section, and came to his seat from the other side. I saw them laughing about it as he went. Big deal—the money that makes people act like that!

And when a man takes that money and tries to buy friends with it, or keep himself young with it, or run the church with it, or do vengeance with it, or substitute for loving his children with it, or pay the wages of his guilt with it—surely God laughs.

Christianity began as a poor man's faith. A richer man can only share it if his heart is right, and his eyes are wide open to the values God assigns. This is what the Scripture says: "A man's life does not consist in the abundance of his possessions" (Luke 12:15). The gospel further admonishes every man "not to think of himself more highly than he ought to think, but to think with sober judgment" (Rom. 12:3). To do this, it may help to hear God laughing now and then.

Finally, I think we must know that *God laughs at all our foolish pride.* Pride has many forms, but three of them are especially important here.

Nationalism is one. Reinhold Niebuhr described it when he said: "The egotism of racial, national and socio-economic groups is most consistently expressed by a national state . . . . The temptation to idolatry is implicit in the state's majesty." Niebuhr also warned that "no politically crystallized social group has, therefore, ever existed without entertaining, or succumbing to, the temptation of making idolatrous claims for itself." [8]

Jesus told us to "Render to Caesar the things that are Caesar's, and to God the things that are God's" (Mark 12:17). The problem is that we're easily led to confuse those issues, to blur the distinctions, and we end up rendering to some Caesar the things which belong to God alone.

The slogan which leads us there is the one which says "my country right or wrong." As someone once said, that's a little like saying "my grandfather, drunk or sober." And there's also something in it which sounds a lot like Isaiah's description of Babylon:

*You felt secure in your wickedness, you said, "No one sees me"; your wisdom and your knowledge led you astray, and you said in your heart, "I am, and there is no one besides me"* (Isa. 47:10). Doesn't that describe a society whose national pride has led it to declare a virtual infallibility, to feel secure in its illusions of grandeur, and to deny the existence of any higher court of judgment than its own tribunals? Surely God laughs at such a foolish pride of nationalism.

Another one of pride's expressions is that of racism. He who sits in the heavens "made all of us earth-dwellers of one blood" (see Acts 17:26). And with him "There is neither Jew nor Greek, there is neither slave nor free, there is neither male nor female; for you are all one in Christ Jesus" (Gal. 3:28).

Over and over in the Bible, God says to us: "You're all the same; you're *all* my children." But in our silly pride, we keep denying that. We say we're *not* the same. My race, my group, my color—we're different. We're God's favorites, and those strangers are something else.

Jesus himself encountered that. Though he was a Jew by birth, he refused to participate in their hatred of the Samaritans. So do you know what they said about him? "Why you're not one of us; you're one of those dirty Samaritans" (see John 4:48). Of course, that wasn't the first racial slur, and certainly not the last. In fact, no race that ever lived on earth has escaped being the *object* of it, or of *participating* in it.

It's time we learned that racial pride and racial hatred are partners, and that both are equally foolish, unreasonable, and wicked.

There is another expression of our pride which God must surely laugh at on occasion. I became aware of it as I sat in one of our national religious conventions with about twelve thousand other people. Over and over I heard a word used—a simple word, a common word, but in its constant usage, a very revealing word. It was the word *"great."* Our *great* convention, our *great*

24

president, our *great* program, our *great* heritage, our *great* churches, our *great* doctrines, our *great* institutions—over and over, up and down, backward and forward, the message was clear. We think we're something great! God surely is lucky to have us on his side!

It made me think of J. D. Salinger's novel, *The Catcher in the Rye,* and of Holden Caulfield's visit to a Christmas celebration in Radio City Music Hall. Holden observed all the trumped-up religious paradings, all the show business sentimentality, and in a coarse vernacular he said to his girl friend: "Good old Jesus would have puked at the sight." John Killinger, the Vanderbilt professor, has a good comment on that passage. He says: "Blasphemers are so often right, because they are not taken in by the small pieties most of us fall prey to." [9]

Dare we, then, to raise the question: "Has God laughed at some of us?" Our inflated claims to goodness, our little hoards of what we call wealth, the foolishness of a pride which we substitute for true devotion—are these the objects of his scorn?

How can we find, instead, the smile of his approval? It has to do with integrity. Here is what a magnificent Old Testament passage says about it: *If you receive my words and treasure up my commandments with you, making your ear attentive to wisdom and inclining your heart to understanding; yes, if you cry out for insight and raise your voice for understanding, if you seek it like silver and search for it as for hidden treasures; then you will understand the fear of the Lord and find the knowledge of God. . . . For the Lord gives wisdom; from his mouth come knowledge and understanding; he stores up sound wisdom for the upright; as a shield to those who walk in integrity"* (Prov. 2:1–7).

# 3

# Why I Am Not a Christian

All of you know a man like this: secular, well-educated, perceptive, articulate. After being in and out of several churches, he finally became somewhat of a critic, although he does a lot of community things like voter registrations and Cancer Society fund raising. You feel a little uncomfortable around him, because you always wonder if he's analyzing you or not. He's sort of a "letters to the editor" type, if you know what I mean.

I'm sure he doesn't get many invitations to speak in churches, and when you hear him you'll know why. [10] You may not like what he says, and please know that I don't agree with all of it myself. But I think we ought to hear a man like this, because it's the best hope of seeing ourselves as an outsider sees us.

The real question the world is asking about us Christians isn't what we think it is. It's not about our doctrines, although that would be nice. It's not where we stand on issues, although that's important. It's not how friendly we are, or how big we are, or how clever we are. The basic question is this: "Are you real or are you phony?"

That's why we need to listen to our critics. It's not that they're always right in what they say about us. It's that they have an angle on our phoniness—they see us like we can't see ourselves—and this can be an aid to integrity if we'll let it. Integrity begins with a capacity for self-judgment. If we're not willing to hear criticism, to answer questions, to "meet the press"—embarrassing as that may sometimes be—then we're not ready to take our gospel to the marketplace.

I admired John F. Kennedy for that. Week after week, good times or rough times, he walked into that press room and exposed himself to questions. *Mr. President, I'd like to know something. . . . Mr. President, why did you do that? . . . Mr. President, what do you plan to do about this?* Now I'm not saying that this guarantees integrity, but I'm saying it helps. And if we avoid it, if we stay barricaded behind closed doors, if we communicate only through proclamations issued by press agents or other intermediaries, if we keep ourselves surrounded by smiling praise-tellers, if we forbid the page of the critic from coming in to disturb our illusions, then credibility not only suffers, it dies without hope of redemption.

So let's listen. Good things happen when you listen. Hear a man out; let him have his say. There's hope in that, for him and for us.

*This is very strange to me: being here in this church, listening to you sing, seeing your lovely stained glass, the Bible, the cross. I suppose most of you come here for this every Sunday. Well, I tried that for awhile, but it didn't work out for me.*

*I hope you know why I'm here this morning. And I certainly hope you don't blame the pastor for what I say. He asked me to tell you how I feel about some things. You see, I'm not a Christian, and I'm going to tell you why.*

*It's not that religion is harmful, it's that it's so harmless—so silent and invisible, so off-to-the-side, so nonpublic. Churches are little retreats where people get away and forget about the world. It doesn't hurt anything, but it's so irrelevant and wasteful.*

*One Black Panther member is worth a hundred Christians as far as bringing social change is concerned. The church just isn't on the growing edge. It's not even part of the discussion. The place where the future's coming from is the government agency, the university, the labor union, and groups like women's rights, consumer affairs, health care, and environment. The churches are*

27

*obviously afraid of being part of those discussions, because* *they're afraid of the disagreement that always goes along with it. And so, if they do speak out on issues occasionally, it's always something that's been pretty well settled—safe territory.*

*It's really a planned irrelevance, as I see it. And I think I know why. Your church is a society for the preservation of illusions. You have an illusion you're doing mission work—winning the world to Christ!—when actually you're becoming more extinct with each generation. You have an illusion that getting people coming to Sunday School and church makes them a lot better than others, and it doesn't at all. You have an illusion that giving away a few old clothes and Christmas baskets is really meeting the needs of the poor, and that's a laugh!*

*I'll tell you something else that's a laugh. It's when those semireligious politicians, and those semipolitical religionists, get together for their prayer breakfasts and White House worship services. You hear all their flattery and pious talk. Then you read those transcripts and hear them cursing God behind closed doors, and you know it was all for show. What honest man would want a religion like that?*

*Most of your ministers aren't any better. They're all seeking their own comfort and acceptance. They're out for glamor and gifts. Like some third-rate movie actor, they will take any part to please the congregation and get along in the hierarchy. The only trouble you ever hear of one getting into is moral trouble. So where's all this courage and boldness you sing about in those hymns?*

*What I'm saying is this: I'd be a lot more interested in Christianity if it weren't for the Christians I know and read about. How do all you people know you're not just fooling yourselves, and wasting a lot of time and money playing church?*

*What does your faith amount to except just believing what you've been told? You haven't really thought it through. You haven't really searched out reasons for things. And then you*

28

*wonder why it's hard to get your bright teenagers and college students to follow it. Just ask them; they'll tell you.*

*You see, I'm a person who reasons things out. It's against my nature to accept things without proof. So tell me, how can you prove God? I know a lot of people look at the world and say the flowers and trees and mountains speak of God. But what about those others things—those ugly, miserable things? What do they speak of? I was in the army. I fought in that war, and I can't forget that. Where do you find God in cities being bombed, people being blown to bits, or burned alive? If there is a God who has all power and really loves us, why would he let things like that happen?*

*Think of all the crime we have, all the terrible diseases, all the tragedies—I know some people deserve what happens to them, but so many don't. So many fine, decent, and totally innocent people suffer all kinds of pain. Why? Can you tell me why?*

*But even that isn't my biggest problem. The biggest is the people I know who claim to be Christians. I can't tell that they're any better than I am, or that their children are any better than mine. I can't see that they do any more to help others.*

*Well, let me just ask you; why are there so few of you who'll do anything more than just come to church and sit? How many of you really go out of your way, really sacrifice anything, really assume any more obligation than belonging to some kind of club? You claim the Christian faith makes a difference, that it's a way of life; but can you show me what difference it's made in you?*

*And then I hear churches planning to take this to other countries! Well, who would want it? And if Christians don't care any more than they seem to about the people who live in this country, who would think they'd care very much about people living way off? I've read about churches who sent missionaries to the black people in Africa, but they won't even speak to the black people who live right around them, much less accept them into membership.*

29

Let me ask you something else. What about all those people who belong to your church and never even attend? Are they Christians or not? If they are, then your salvation must not make much of a difference, because it certainly doesn't make much to them. If you say they're not really Christians, then why aren't you doing something about it? They're on your church rolls.

I suppose it all comes down to this: I'm not a Christian because I can live a very good life without it. I'd rather not claim so much, and then end up doing more than I claim. To me, that's better than claiming everything a man can dream of, like you Christians do, and ending up doing so very little.

Still . . . still, I'll have to say honestly that although I've never been able to believe in God completely, I've never been able to disbelieve completely either. I don't accept your faith, but I'm not happy in doubt either. I'm not at all sure you Christians have found the answers, but I'm still looking, too. And I'm not completely satisfied with my life. I'd like to find something more.

It's strange. Since I've been telling you all this, I've been thinking that all these years since Christ lived, there've always been Christians—it's kept on going. It seems like it would have just died out, and people forgotten all about it. That really bothers me, because for something to last two thousand years— people still building buildings, and writing books, and spending all this time and effort with it—it does seem like that shows there's something to it.

Oh, now, listen, don't you think I'm admitting anything! If God's in the church today, he must be hidden mighty well. I'm a fair-minded person; I've looked at all the evidence. And for the most part, I'm not impressed.

I'm not impressed with your crowds, or your expensive buildings, or your preachers, or all those activities you're so busy with. I can explain all that, and I can explain all those things you argue about God.

The only thing I really can't explain is this man I know. He is so *very happy and well-adjusted. I know the job he does—he's a safety inspector—and that job's enough to drive two people crazy. But he's always smiling, always calm, always saying nice things to people, even when they give him a hard time.*

*That little church he belongs to just couldn't live without him. He's put his whole life into it, and yet he never brags or asks for praise. I suppose you call that humility. But whatever it is, I don't know anyone who doesn't notice how dedicated he is, but how little he asks in return. And I don't know where a man gets the stuff to go on like that.*

*His wife died a year or so ago, and I'll never forget how he took it with such grace. Call it courage or faith or whatever, it really impressed me.*

*I've never heard that man say an unkind word. I don't think there's a particle of deceit or pride or dishonesty about him. He's real. And if all the Christians I know were like that man, I guess I'd already be one myself.*

*That's all I have to say . . . .*

# Part II

## Integrity in Religion

Dear Pastor, Sir:

You probably won't remember me. I'm the guy with the mustache who usually sits near the outside aisle on row nineteen. I used to shake hands with you as I left the church. But you kept thinking I was a visitor, and that embarrassed both of us. So lately I just slip out the side door.

I know you're a busy man. And I know it must take a lot of time to study for those fine sermons you preach. I guess you must have hundreds of phone calls—you're on so many committees, and director of so many projects. In fact, sir, all the members say we're fortunate to have a pastor who's so successful in the ministry.

There's just one thing that's bothering me. If the church is really supposed to be a fellowship of love, how come no one ever notices me? I've been coming for a year now, and all I ever got was a pledge card and a box of offering envelopes.

# 4

## Wash Your Face

*A man of the world he was, that Jesus. He wasn't a religious man by the standards of our day. It was very strange to us that he should be known as a religious leader, because he was always associating with the wrong people and expressing doubts about sacred things like fasting and tithing and the sabbath. He was a radical—a dangerous man.*

*He poked fun at the robes of our priests; he admired the Samaritans; and he spoke disrespectfully of the Temple.*

*He spent his time out in the wilderness alone, or with a group of children, or with the publicans and sinners. There was a lot of talk about that, and he didn't even seem to care.*

*He just never learned the art of making friends with the right people and doing what was expected. No one ever doubted that he was a sensitive young man. If only he could have been satisfied to settle down and act like a rabbi should.*

*It was a shame what happened to him—a real shame.*

Isn't that what one of them might have said—one of those Pharisees he clashed with so often? They were always thinking up ways to be more religious, and he kept advising people to be less religious. "Let everyone see your devotion to God," they said. "Beware of practicing your piety before men," he said. "Go out and pray where crowds will see you," they advised. "Hide in a closet and do it alone," Jesus replied. "Keep the fast so that all can see you and speak of your devotion." "No," says Jesus, "fast if you want to. But don't make a show of it. Comb your hair; dress up; wash your face!" (See Matt. 6:17.)

You see, the Pharisees didn't fast for too long—just from sunrise to sunset. And hunger certainly doesn't begin to show on a person in that short time. So they would go with their faces unwashed to have a drawn look. Sometimes they would also put ashes on their heads, and perhaps rub a little around the eyes to make it look even better! The law required only five or six fasts a year, but the Pharisees went farther than that. They fasted twice a week, as one of them tells us in Luke 18:12. Thursday and Monday were the days they chose, remembering the days Moses went up Mt. Sinai and came back again. Those were also market days in town, and lots of people would be there to see them.

*Oh, look there, children! That man's fasting; can't you see? Shhsh, be quiet. Let's not disturb him. He's a holy man. I think I've seen him here before.*

The man pretends not to hear; that's part of the game. But he does hear those whispered remarks, and he collects them like autographs, because this is really why he came. The important thing is to *seem* religious, to keep up the appearance. What's seen in the window is what counts; what goes on in the back rooms doesn't matter. It's an act, a show, an ego trip in the name of God.

*What's with you, man? Why are you sitting there so sad looking? What good's it doing anyone but you? If these people admire you, so what? You could be doing something useful for others instead of gathering all this admiration. I'd call that serving God, but this is something else.*

Jesus despised such put-on piety. Read the twenty-third chapter of Matthew's gospel if you want to see how strongly he felt about it. There you find a scalding passage about those who did all their deeds to be seen of men, who made their phylacteries broad and their fringes long, and loved the seats of honor and the holy titles which went with them. (See Matt. 23:1–7.)

Jesus compared that kind of religion to a platter which has

been washed clean and sparkling on the outside, but left dirty and rancid on the inside. Who would like to eat out of that? What questions does that half-washed platter raise?

Here are a few of its questions: What good is it to repeat words of praise if your heart is far away? What good does it do pretending before men, when God knows your motive is selfish? What good does it do to practice the trivia of religion when you neglect its true essence? What good is a dark countenance? If your fasting hasn't brought you peace with God, why not wash your face and start all over?

Remember that sabbath when Jesus and his men walked through the fields and made the religious people mad by eating the grain they found? (See Mark 2:23–28.) This brazen act wasn't like those healings he had performed on the sabbath. It wasn't something that *had* to be done. The ox certainly wasn't in the ditch here, so why on earth did the Master do it? I think he did it in absolute rebellion and contempt for any religion which makes service to God such a silly, shallow thing.

Do you remember the story of Ananias and Sapphira in the book of Acts? (5:1–11). Members of the church were selling their houses and lands and using the money for helping the poor. This strange couple couldn't bear doing that. They loved their money too much. But neither could they bear not to *seem* as dedicated as the others. Since it was the *appearance* that mattered, they sold their property, but lied about the price, and kept back part of it. They met their doom trying to behave as expected without meaning it. Had they simply and honestly admitted unwillingness, I think God and the church could have accepted it. It was the deceit, the pretense, the lying dishonesty which made it so terrible.

We'd all like to hear pleasant truth. But even the unpleasant truth is preferable to lying deception. Our country is sick with that—lying deception. Can't we find some honest men and women on whose word we can rely, who'll just tell us the truth and forget the public relations? We need to be leveled with instead of being played with. We need to wash our faces. Governors, senators, economists—do you hear that? Advertisers, lawyers, insurance companies—do you hear that? Mr. President, do you hear it? Potential candidates, do you hear it?

We all need to hear it. Because the religion of today is also in need of washing its face. Of course we don't wear long robes or put ashes on our heads, but we have our own hypocrisies, our own inconsistencies, our own spiritual cover-ups.

We're still inclined to turn the other way on social issues. At a junior high school where my wife taught, the play *Oliver* was given one evening. It was done extremely well. The play shows the oppression of children, which Dickens remembers from his childhood in nineteenth century England. People's responses to that hardship—bad and good alike—are shown. According to the principal, a local pastor was in his office the very next morning, protesting the play because it had scenes where drinking was depicted. According to the principal, the man said nothing of the stealing and murder, which were also depicted. And more importantly, he showed absolutely no appreciation for the valuable social lessons which the performance taught. Where we've been so piously narrow, we need to wash our faces.

Where we've avoided the important issues of our day—racial injustice, truth in government, the rights of women, the peace of the world, the elimination of poverty, and the ecological crisis, including the population explosion (to name just a few)—we need to wash our faces. For it's quick and easy to avoid these problems by busying ourselves with trivia and calling it our religious duty.

Another problem we have is confusing Christ with culture. Some years ago Senator Mark Hatfield addressed a National Prayer Breakfast and spoke of this. He spoke of the "misplaced allegiance, if not outright idolatry" of failing to distinguish between "the God of an American civic religion and the God who reveals himself in the holy scriptures and in Jesus Christ." He warned against appealing to "the god of civil religion . . . a small and exclusive deity, a defender of only the American nation, the object of a national folk religion devoid of moral content." He said that "those who follow Christ will more often find themselves, not with comfortable majorities, but with miserable minorities." [1]

Another need for face-washing is found in the way we treat our fellowman locally, especially those of a different "culture level." A large hospital where I used to visit regularly had a special parking area for doctors and ministers. A workingman stood guard at the entrance to make sure no one else used it. He knew most of the faces, and he knew mine. But one fateful day I appeared on a motorcycle, wearing coveralls, a helmet, and dark glasses. His greeting was an angry wave. "Hey, boy," he said, "get that thing out of here." You see, he didn't know he was hollering at the Reverend Dr. Briggs! But I thought later, after it was all fixed up, about the people who get hollered at and have no recourse, because it's no mistake.

Why should we think of a teacher or a doctor or an attorney as necessarily being any better than a cab driver or a mechanic or a farmer? Doesn't the church foster and participate in some of that hypocrisy? If we do, we need to wash our faces.

Washing our faces would also mean that we refuse to make substitutions for righteousness. All of us want to be religious, but the way is hard and narrow. We're not anxious for things like sacrifice and pain and toil and repentance. So we begin to make little substitutions. We get up a little creed, and say it to one another. We make ourselves critics of others, and we substitute those criticisms for our personal obedience—acting as if we're lifting up ourselves when we put others down. Or maybe we retreat into our history—we talk about how we *used* to serve, or how godly our parents were. And we do this to avoid thinking about the fact that we're not living it now.

Washing our faces would also mean to quit pretending to be so sure of everything. A church leader I once knew was very sure God intended the group to buy a certain piece of property. He had prayed about it, and it had been revealed to him that this was what the Almighty intended. Anyone who questioned the purchase was questioning the will of God. But unfortunately, God seemed unable to convince the Urban Planning Commission of it, and they awarded the property to the telephone company! Pretending we're right about everything, pretending God is always on our side, pretending we have all the answers—right here is another place we need to wash our faces.

Howard Butt has written a book called *The Velvet Covered Brick*, and I found a paragraph there which really speaks to this issue of personal authenticity. He said: "I used to worry because 'evil' people seemed more interesting to me than 'good' people—more fascinating, more alive, more gripping. Pale, 'churchly' people bored me; wild, 'reckless' people charmed me: between an X-rated and a G-rated movie I'd have known without checking which would have been the most exciting. Now I understand my confusion. 'Evil' people are at least *real*; I responded not to their evil but to their *reality*. It is easier to be really evil than to be really good. Real evil always whips phony goodness. Real self-centeredness, fake or real, religious or profane, cannot compare to the life centered in God: you come alive." [2] Washing your face—that's what he's talking about.

If we would do that, we could at last confess our sins; we could express our doubts; we could talk about our problems; we could admit our mistakes; we could face some real issues. In the process, we could also join the human race. And in so doing, we could also be better Christians—less religious perhaps, but more Christian.

So don't look dismal like the hypocrites! They have their reward. Anoint your head, and wash your face! Be yourself; be honest; no matter what it costs. Be devoted, not to the god of outward appearance, but to the God of the secret place.

# 5

## Insiders Outside; Outsiders Inside

No one quite knows why, but early in his ministry, Jesus left his hometown of Nazareth for a much larger city called "Capernaum by the sea" (Matt. 4:13). It's the only place in the four Gospels where he was ever said to be "at home" (Mark 2:1). It was also the town of Peter and Andrew, and it was a place where many of his miracles were performed. There Jesus healed a man right in the midst of the synagogue, and received a lot of criticism, because he did it on the sabbath.

One of the most enlightening stories from Capernaum is the one in chapter 8 of Matthew's Gospel, where Christ heals the servant of a Roman army officer. The man's servant is sick and dying; but full of hope, he comes to Christ and asks for help. "I'll go at once," says Jesus. "You don't need to do that," the centurion answers. "Just say the word. Your word is all that's needed. I understand about words, you see. I give commands too. I believe you have the authority; so just say the word" (See Matt. 8:7–9).

Even though the man was a Gentile, a soldier, and a secular man, Jesus found much to commend in his attitude. "Even among those religious people who fill the synagogues, I didn't find faith like this," he says. Their faith was the prideful, self-serving kind. But this centurion had actually declined Jesus' offer to come to his house, saying he wasn't worthy to have Jesus come under his roof. Was this some act? Not worthy? Apparently not, for Jesus finds more to please God here than in all the religious pomp he was used to seeing where the candles burned and men wore long robes.

The Master made a penetrating analysis here: this centurion was an "outsider" to the scribes and Pharisees, but Jesus claimed he had more true religion than they did—those "insiders," as they thought of themselves. And Jesus foresees a day when God will make this judgment known. Those "insiders" will be outside, and "outsiders," such as this army man, will be inside. *I tell you, many will come from east and west and sit at table with Abraham, Isaac, and Jacob in the kingdom of heaven, while the sons of the kingdom will be thrown into the outer darkness; there men will weep and gnash their teeth* (Matt. 8:11–12).

Now, admittedly, that's not the kind of passage you hear many sermons on. But I realized, as I studied it, that there are others like it in the teachings of Christ. So I searched and found a sizable number. Their importance is that they devastate the arrogance of institutional religion. For the smug assumption of institutional religion is that it has a special claim on the membership of the kingdom. Jesus questioned that on several occasions.

In Luke, chapter 13, the question is asked: "Lord, will those who are saved be few?" And Jesus replies: *Strive to enter by the narrow door; for many, I tell you, will seek to enter and will not be able. When once the householder has risen up and shut the door, you will begin to stand outside and to knock at the door, saying, "Lord, open to us." He will answer you, "I do not know where you came from." Then you will begin to say, "We ate and drank in your presence, and you taught in our streets." But he will say, "I tell you, I do not know where you come from; depart from me, all you workers of iniquity." There you will weep and gnash your teeth, when you see Abraham and Isaac and Jacob and all the prophets in the kingdom of God, and you yourselves thrust out. And men will come from east and west, and from north and south, and sit at the table in the kingdom of God. And behold, some are last who will be first, and some are first who will be last* (vv. 22–30).

Doesn't that passage mean that a lot of religious "insiders" may someday be left out? Didn't Christ once say to a group of them that the tax collectors and harlots were going into the kingdom before them? Long-haired kids, black radicals, welfare mothers, homosexuals, and massage parlor operators—going to God ahead of regular, churchgoing people? How can that possibly be? What about all the tithes I've paid? And now he says that someone else may take my place!

What if we were told that some communists were going into the kingdom of God before us? I read a letter from a Baptist leader in Rumania which spoke of changes in that country, making it easier to spread the Christian faith. The letter stated that after years of atheistic materialism, many communists were turning to God. The leader considered such lands as more fertile soil for Christian missions than is America. America, he said, is just as materialistic, but we practice it in the name of God. What if the man turned out to be right? What would it mean? Just this: Insiders outside; outsiders inside.

What if you told conservative Protestants that Roman Catholics were going into the kingdom of God before them? Dead ritual, scriptural error, bondage to a human dictator, a lot of plain superstition—that's what Protestants have said about the Catholic church. But something different is taking place today. Changes are occurring which make you wonder where the spirit of the reformers really is. And the boundary line between inside and outside has become so crooked and wandering that it's really no line at all.

There are other New Testament passages about insiders and outsiders. One of them is in the Gospel of Luke, chapter 11. *The men of Nineveh will arise at the judgment with this generation and condemn it; for they repented at the preaching of Jonah, and behold, something greater than Jonah is here* (Luke 11:32). Jesus is here comparing two kinds of people, and their response to the gospel. The Nineveh-dwellers were "outsiders." Yet, they found

45

faith through an angry sermon delivered by a disturbed prophet. By contrast the people of Judea heard the gospel from the Messiah himself and turned it aside. In the judgment, says Jesus, those "outsiders" will be inside and those "insiders" will be outside.

Even the parable of the good Samaritan has this idea underlying it. Those first men who came down that road—the priest and the Levite—were "insiders." They were religious men, perhaps on their way to worship that very hour. Yet they were too busy to help the unfortunate traveler who lay by the road. They passed on by in a hurry. Then along came an "outsider," a Samaritan, an unholy man by their standards. And this man gave his time, his effort, his money, his transportation, his compassion. Doesn't Jesus make it plain that to such he will say "come ye blessed," and to the others, "depart from me"? *Insiders outside; outsiders inside!*

What about this story? *Two men went up into the temple to pray, one a Pharisee and the other a tax collector. The Pharisee stood and prayed thus with himself. "God, I thank thee that I am not like other men, extortioners, unjust, adulterers, or even like this tax collector. I fast twice a week; I give tithes of all that I get." But the tax collector, standing far off, would not even lift up his eyes to heaven, but beat his breast, saying, "God, be merciful to me a sinner!" I tell you, this man went down to his house justified rather than the other* (Luke 18:10–14).

It's easy to identify insiders and outsiders here, isn't it? The Pharisee is so sure of his position with God. He's proud, conservative, strict. The outsider—that tax collector—is a worldly man, an outcast of society. Not at all sure of his standing with God, he brings only his deep need, and a desire to be heard. And God hears that man, but turns a deaf ear to the other one.

The next story almost speaks for itself: A farmer rents his land and goes on a long journey. While he's gone, the renters turn against him and waste his land. Look at what the Scripture says then: *When therefore the owner of the vineyard comes, what will he do to those tenants? They said to him, "He will put those wretches to a miserable death, and let out the vineyard to other tenants who will give him the fruits in their season." Jesus said to them, . . . Therefore I tell you, the kingdom of God will be taken away from you and given to a nation producing the fruits of it"* (Matt. 21:40–43).

There's a certain disquietude in reading those passages. After all, I'm a minister—a religious professional. I'm a holy man; I'm an insider! I mainly meet with insiders and associate with insiders. Has this made me proud? Do I despise others? Do I think of God as a possession of mine, or am I a possession of his? Could it be that most of us "insiders" are far too comfortable, too assured, too prone to take God for granted?

Please don't miss the point. I'm not saying that all the good people are bad, and all the bad people are really good. And I'm not seeking to weaken anyone's faith, but to strengthen it by prompting a reexamination—especially if it has arrogance or presumption in it. To assist in this reexamination, let me seek to draw some proper conclusions from the study we have made.

First, *we must recognize the dreadful offense of spiritual pride.* I used to sometimes hear a so-called gospel song which asked about who would get to heaven, then it answered by chanting: "If anybody makes it, surely I will." *Get my mansion ready, Lord, Here I come! Just hang my robe and crown in the hall closet please! And, oh, yes, save a good seat for me around the table. That big one at your right hand will do.*

I can almost hear the words: *Why call ye me Lord, Lord, and do not the things which I say?* (Luke 6:46, KJV). Or those others: Let him that thinketh he standeth take heed lest he fall (1 Cor. 10:12, KJV). Or those others: *Let nothing be done through strife or vainglory; but in lowliness of mind let each esteem others better than himself* (Phil. 2:3).

Religious showmanship is very popular and tempting today,

just as it has always been. Religious pride is very ego-pumping today, just as it's always been. The threat of a secularized world is very great, but the greatest threat the church faces today is the misguided zeal of overreligious people. When people have been raised on frozen orange juice concentrate, they're likely to think a glass of freshly squeezed juice is artificial! In the same way, a man can become so used to an artificial religious experience that he will not recognize the new and living way when he sees it practiced before his eyes. [3]

In the second place, *our faith must rest in God's revealed truth and not upon man's traditions.* A lot of people continue to suppose that salvation comes through joining a certain church and accepting its doctrines. Many think that walking down some aisle in response to a public invitation is all that's needed. But you can join a dozen churches—you can walk down the aisle till you wear out the rug—and still not be saved. That comes through a personal encounter which defies an assembly line approach. Yet, in its arrogance, institutional religion will keep offering it in creeds, church letters, baptisms, good workers, and a respectable appearance of being religious.

The Pharisee felt comfortable with his god, because he had lowered the risk of faith to a religiosity which meant little but could be easily kept. It also gave him a quick, easy way to distinguish between insiders and outsiders, and to pass the package onto his children. The lesson for us is not to avoid religion, but to avoid its arrogance, and to seek it firsthand, not through some pious intermediary.

Then, finally, I think this talk of insiders and outsiders should *change our spirit, and lead us to follow Christ in reverence, humility, and fear.* Paul spoke of that when he wrote to the Christians in Rome. He recognized they had taken Israel's place of favor with God, but he warns them not to presume on that favor. *But if some of the branches were broken off, and you, a wild olive shoot, were grafted in their place to share the richness* of the olive tree, do not boast over the branches. If you do boast, remember it is not you that support the root, but the root that supports you. You will say, "Branches were broken off so that I might be grafted in." That is true. They were broken off because of their unbelief, but you stand fast only through faith. So do not become proud, but stand in awe. For if God did not spare the natural branches, neither will he spare you (Rom. 11:17–21).

"Do not *boast* . . . do not be *proud* . . . but *stand in awe*." Don't act like most insiders do! Instead, remember that Christ is your life, and you must continue in union with him or you die.

A great deal of Scripture has been quoted already, but one other passage may serve to summarize a proper response to God. The writer of the book of Hebrews recalls the unfaithfulness of those insiders who left Egypt for the Promised Land. He shows God's displeasure that they had forsaken the destiny he chose for them. He then turns to us and warns: *Take care, brethren, lest there be in any of you an evil, unbelieving heart, leading you to fall away from the living God. But exhort one another every day, as long as it is called "today," that none of you may be hardened by the deceitfulness of sin. For we share in Christ, if only we hold our first confidence firm to the end. Therefore, while the promise of entering his rest remains, let us fear lest any of you be judged to have failed to reach it* (Heb. 3:12–14; 4:1).

What does it mean to fear God? What meaning has that ancient term for us moderns? Well, it means we fear to be without him, and we don't presume on that. We fear we do not love him enough. We fear we may dishonor his holy name. We fear to disobey his Word.

I'd like to get a little more of that fear in the church today. Where we've made a secure and exclusive haven out of our religion, we need it shattered so we'll be free to know the love of God firsthand. It's only then, in that presence, we find the peace we sought so prematurely, and settled for so cheaply.

God does want all of us inside, and he gives each of us that opportunity. "This is eternal life, that they know thee the only true God, and Jesus Christ whom thou has sent" (John 17:3). And someday all those who accept that offered gift will come from east and west and north and south, and sit at table in the kingdom of heaven.

# 6

## The Difference Between Holiness and Self-righteousness

There's an old Arab proverb which advises that if your neighbor makes a pilgrimage to Mecca, watch him. If he makes two pilgrimages, avoid him. And if he makes three, move to another street!

That proverb raises a perplexing question for religious people of all persuasions. Simply stated it is this: The more religious you become, the more you're suspected of faking it. Your search for piety seems counterproductive; the more authentic you try to become, the less authentic you seem to others.

That can be illustrated by the uncertainty you sometimes face as you receive food in a public restaurant. If you bow your head and give thanks to God, you feel like the man in the Arab proverb. People will watch you, and perhaps even avoid you. At best, they'll misunderstand you. But if you avoid the prayer, you may feel guilty and ungrateful, for sometimes you remember that God is watching too.

Jesus mentioned this problem on more than one occasion. He warned his disciples against practicing their piety before men, to be seen by them (Matt. 6:1–8). He made scornful fun of those whose main intent centered around the impressions they made on others. He even called them "hypocrites": a word which originally came from Greek drama, and described one who plays a part.

Yet, in spite of these warnings against cosmetic religion, Jesus also told his followers to be like a "city set on a hill"—for men to

51

see, of course. He told them to be the "light of the world," and to let that light shine before men "that they may *see* your good works and give glory to your Father who is in heaven" (Matt. 5:16). This leaves us the task of knowing the difference between holiness and self-righteousness. How can we be the truly devout, holy person Jesus commended, without having the artificial self-righteousness he warned about so often?

The more you are involved in religious life, the more of a problem that becomes. And when you're a minister, it arises almost daily. The Bob Newhart Show did a story about a middle-aged pastor who was especially troubled with this. In an unforgettable scene, the man comes to Bob's office to discuss his misery. Carol, Bob's unsuspecting secretary, knows the man only as a pleasant, well-dressed American male. And she responds accordingly, until the terrible truth is suddenly revealed—he's a minister! After that, the poor man is treated with exaggerated respect. And Carol even dons an overcoat to cover her short skirt, which suddenly has become a great embarrassment! Soon afterward, the man announces to a bewildered congregation that he is leaving the ministry.

This is not a contention that all the men with integrity leave the ministry, and only the hypocrites remain. But one must recognize with Charles Merrill Smith, that religious work *does* place a premium on show and sham and insincerity—that self-righteousness may often be rewarded, where holiness gets in the way. [4] And though this problem is illustrated more clearly in the life of a clergyman, every conscientious layman has it too.

Could it be that much of what we call holiness is really just self-righteousness, as God observes it? Could it be that much of our religious activity is no better than the actions of those who sounded the trumpets as they prayed on street corners, or disfigured their faces to glamorize the effect of their fasting?

One of the best compliments I ever received came from an old farmer in a country church I served as a college student. The time had come to leave and go away to seminary. People in rural areas don't say a lot on occasions like that. But this fellow braced himself up, looked me in the eye, and said: "Well, Preacher, I'll say this for ya: As long as I've knowed ya there warn't no put-on about ya." By "put-on," he meant artificiality. And that was a real compliment, because rural people are pretty shrewd judges of that. I'd like to be worthy of it, but the problem is that if we're not constantly aware of creeping hypocrisy, all of us will have this problem.

Consider the story of the Pharisee and publican who went up to pray in the Temple. Take what the Pharisee said and did, and try it on for fit. Then do the same with the publican. The troubling thing is that most of us are much more comfortable with the role of the Pharisee—with his words and thoughts and attitude—than that of the other.

How often do we confess our sins like the publican did? How often do we really feel unworthy in the presence of God? Don't we often sit back, look critically at others, and feel glad we're not like them? Aren't we much more comfortable finding fault, than looking at ourselves?

I once asked a retreat group to do the following exercise: Those over thirty, write a confession of how you have contributed to the generation gap: those under thirty, do the same. When we came back together for discussion, something very revealing occurred. In no more than two minutes, each group had begun to defend itself and blame the other. Each avoided the self-examination and confession which could lead to holiness, and chose instead the self-justification which could only lead to an inflated self-righteousness.

Let's come back to that question of how you tell the difference between the two. I would propose three tests: First of all, *holiness seeks to obey God, and doesn't really care so much about men; but self-righteousness seeks to please men, and doesn't really care so much about God.*

It's a lot like dieting. There are two kinds of dieting: honest dieting and "table dieting." The first means you're consistent with it, whether anyone is watching or not. But "table dieting" means saying you're on a diet—gaining admiration, passing up food in front of others—then making up for it by eating on the sly. Sometime in the afternoon, you stop at this little place on the corner. Or you snack on some things you've hidden in your desk, or slip into the refrigerator and feast on the very leftovers you staunchly resisted at mealtime! Now "table dieting" doesn't do much good, does it?

It's the same with God, you see. God our Father knows us—knows if our religion is for show or for real. But it's tempting to make our expressions of faith sound good to others. And we can be so concerned with credit and praise and recognition that it becomes our chief activity.

There's practically no limit to what we can do as churches, *if it doesn't matter who gets the credit.* But where holiness is weak and self-righteousness is strong, one must constantly keep track of who needs to be recognized, who needs to be thanked, and who needs his ego soothed or smoothed. In a more authentic society, people will actually take a little more than their share of blame when things go wrong, and a little less than their share of credit when things go right. And that's what real holiness does, because its aim is to obey God, and get his work done.

Why did the good Samaritan help that unconscious robbery victim he found lying beside the road? There wasn't anyone there to see him do it. That's one of the great lessons of the story. He helped because the man was in need, and he cared. That priest and that Levite who passed on by—what was their problem? Could it be that they were men so accustomed to having an audience, they could see no benefit in helping without it? Could it be that if some people had been there to see and praise—especially some of the elders or members of the ministerial association—they would have rushed to help?

In the second place, *self-righteousness lives in right relation to a moral code, but holiness lives in right relation to other people.* A moral code is good and necessary, but if all a person has is a list of do's and don'ts, they will promptly lead him to self-righteousness. Holiness requires an orientation to the needs of people, toward hurting, toward showing Christian love. An authentic Christian life cannot live on negatives alone.

There was a park in Kentucky where my family and I used to go on occasion. You never saw a place with so many signs telling things not to do. Whoever ran that park was a genius at looking for every place where something out of order could be done and placing a sign there which said not to do it. "Don't walk on the grass; don't park in this space; don't throw trash on the ground; don't leave children unattended; don't let pets run loose; don't make loud noises; don't do this, and don't do that." After awhile, you began to look for one at the gate which said "Don't come into this park!" Because of this, our family name for the place became the "Do-not Park."

I'm convinced that there are a great many "Do-not Christians"—people whose lives are nothing more than a string of prohibitions. And when you add up their goodness, that's all you have left. They won't help you. They won't use their supposed goodness for the benefit of others. They use it, instead, to condemn others and exalt themselves. They may be good in their own sight, but in the sight of God they're good for nothing!

As far back as the Ten Commandments, it was recognized that goodness is *goodness in relation to others.* Six of those ten laws relate to our duty to others, while four speak to our duty to God. And the commandment is not content just to say "do not bear false witness." It says, "You shall not bear false witness *against your neighbor,*" Nor is it content to say "do not covet." It says, "You shall not covet *your neighbor's house*" (or wife, or other property).

St. John of the Cross was a Spanish mystic who labored for

reform of the church in the sixteenth century. He was perse-
cuted, imprisoned, and later excommunicated on the demands of
his enemies. A century and a half later, his piety was recognized
and he was canonized a saint. He was a gentle man who preached
the stern demands of divine love. [5] And he once said: "He who
acts out of pure love of God, not only does he not perform his
actions to be seen of men, but does not do them even that God
may know them. Such a one, if he thought it possible that his
good works might escape the eye of God, would still perform
them with the same Joy, the same Pureness of love." [6] In love
with himself, the self-righteous man has his eye on the rules—
how he can get his reward. But in love with God, the holy man
has his eye on others, how he can share himself with them.

I believe there's also one other appropriate test: *Holiness keeps
company with humility and kindness, while self-righteousness
keeps company with pride and contention.* The holy man sees a
burning bush in the desert, and is struck with awe. He takes off
his shoes, because he knows he stands in the presence of God.
But the self-righteous man sees the bush, and runs off immediately to tell all who will listen how God has blessed and
honored him, and verified his spirituality by giving him this great
experience! Now if what is called the "charismatic movement"
can pass that test, I suppose I can live with it. But if not—if it's a
group of people priding themselves on some special experience,
and judging those who avoid it—I call it a ridiculous way to seek
true holiness.

Holiness keeps company with humility and kindness. Francis
Bacon, the seventeenth-century English statesman, once wrote:
"If a man be gracious and courteous to strangers, it shews he is a
citizen of the world, that his heart is no island cut off from other
lands, but a continent that joins them." [7]

William Law was, in the eighteenth century, one of the most
important English writers on the practical Christian life. He had
a profound effect upon his contemporaries, especially John Wes-

ley and George Whitefield. In his great devotional classic, *A Serious Call to a Devout and Holy Life*, Law described the practical way to personal goodness: "Do not, therefore, please yourself with thinking how piously you would act and submit to God in a plague, a famine, or persecution, but be intent upon the perfection of the present day, and be assured that the best way of showing a true zeal is to make little things the occasion of great piety." [8]

*Little things, the occasion of great piety.* Kindness to little children, and to animals, and to all things weak and helpless. Letting someone pour out all his bitterness on you, until there's none of it left, because you didn't give any of it back. Waving aside the noise of those who say you shouldn't be friends with people "like that," and being a friend anyway—*little things.*

Taking your busy time to teach a class of teenage girls who may not seem to appreciate it; carrying trash around in your pocket because you just can't throw it on the ground, like so many do; praying for some friend in distress at a late-night hour—*little things.* Truthfulness, honesty, virtue—*little things.*

*But in those things, God's Spirit lives and breathes; and though we fear to make the claim ourselves, men know that we are his disciples.*

# Part III

## Integrity in Citizenship and Conduct

Dear Mr. President:

I heard your speech the other day. Not in person, of course. I listened to it on the evening news. You seem to feel the country's in pretty decent shape right now, and that your administration deserves to be reelected.

I want you to know that I'm one of those who voted for you last time. Maybe I will again. But I think there's something you need to know about our country right now. It's just this, sir—no one knows what to believe anymore. Almost every week, we find out we were lied to last week. That keeps us very confused, to say the least.

I'm sorry if the truth doesn't look that good. And I know it leaves you in a tough spot, to think of the blame you get when you tell it. But really, sir, we've had the cover-up treatment way too long. We've been through some rough times before, and I think we could take it again, if we knew the real situation.

Couldn't you just tell your people to be honest with us, and see how it works out?

# 7

## Watergate Isn't Very Far from Here

Watergate isn't very far from here. From suburban Maryland, where our church is located, it's just a few miles. And you have an excellent choice of routes.

The most direct way is down Sixteenth Street, the "Avenue of Churches." As I drove it one day, I counted thirty-nine churches, synagogues, and other religious meeting places. And that doesn't count the large white house you see at the end of the street, where Pennsylvania Avenue comes across. Church services used to be held there, remember? Famous evangelists and ministers would come to speak of high ideals and moral principles. But then, quite suddenly, it all stopped. And now the President who used to live there has moved far away.

Another route to Watergate is down the George Washington Memorial Parkway. There aren't any churches that way, but it's a lovely winding drive—the kind sports cars and motorcycles love—and it does have its reminders. About halfway down, you pass the CIA headquarters, and a little farther on, some over-looks where a former employee, James McCord, met a secret envoy of the White House to discuss executive clemency in exchange for silence. And as you cross the Potomac River later on, you might recall John Ehrlichman's reported suggestion that some sensitive papers from Howard Hunt's safe be dumped there.[1]

But my favorite route is one that lies between these two, through Rock Creek Park. It's amazing there could be such a road in the midst of a city like Washington. No houses, no gas stations, no delivery trucks, no government buildings, no billboards or neon lights or phone booths or hamburger shops—you can almost imagine yourself at Thoreau's Walden Pond or Robert Frost's deserted woods on a snowy evening. It's a restful drive, a place to escape the cares of the world. But, as most things do, it comes to an end. And there, at its end, you find the building known as Watergate.

The Watergate complex is the most valuable, privately owned real estate in Washington. Actually, there are six buildings—a hotel, two office buildings, and three apartment buildings. Some of those apartments have sold for as much as a quarter-million dollars since they were built in the mid-sixties. From their windows you may view the Potomac, the Kennedy Center, the Lincoln Memorial, the White House, and the Capitol.

The Democratic National Committee rented offices on a sixth floor of the Watergate, for the election of 1972. As all the world knows by now, those offices were entered, bugged, and a listening post set up in room 723 of the Howard Johnson Motor Lodge across the street. About two hundred calls were soon monitored. But one of the devices wasn't working well, so a second entry was made on the night of June 16. This was to be the one that failed. A young guard named Frank Wills found some tape on a door and called the police. Three minutes later, some officers in casual clothes answered the call. As they began the search, a lookout across the street came over a walkie-talkie to his boss, Howard Hunt. "Are our people dressed casually, or are they in suits?" Hunt answered that they were in suits. "Well," said Baldwin, "we've got a problem. We've got some people dressed casually, and they've got guns. They're looking around the balcony and everywhere."

Indeed, there was a problem—a problem for those men and their families, a problem for the Committee to Re-Elect the President, a problem for the White House, a problem for the

American voter, a problem to our constitutional system, and a problem for the image of America in the world of nations.

As Americans went to the polls almost six months later, we were still being told, and most believed, that this was an isolated incident, carried out by third-rate burglars—a "panty raid" as one official put it. We were told it had been thoroughly investigated, and that our trusted officials and their staffs had nothing to do with it. But since that time, at least forty-nine persons, including two former attorney generals and fourteen former White House aides or campaign officials, have been convicted or pleaded guilty. Twenty of these men have drawn prison sentences ranging from thirty days to twenty years, and fines of $100 to $40,000. In addition, sixteen other men and sixteen American corporations have been assessed fines of $500 to $35,000. (Since the writing of this book, others may well have joined the list.)

We now are aware that much more than a hotel break-in was involved in the scandal we call Watergate. We are aware that an effort was made to subvert the constitutional election process, and then to cover up that effort. And when all the campaign violations, the operation of the White House "plumbers," the falsifying of the President's income tax papers, the dirty tricks, the illegal contributions, the Ellsberg break-in, and all the rest—when all this is considered, it's not hard to understand why Senator Ervin has called Watergate the greatest tragedy our country ever suffered.

"Let's put Watergate behind us, and get on with the urgent business of the country." We used to hear that a lot, didn't we? "It's over; so let's forget it." "It was unpleasant; let's not talk about it anymore," they used to tell us. I can't agree with that. I feel that even in this late hour, we need to put Watergate in front of us, not behind us, and make it our urgent business to learn why it happened. George Santayana says that those who forget their history are doomed to repeat it. It may not be pleasant to remember that honorable American corporations used unethical and illegal practices in efforts to buy the government for their profit. It may not be pleasant to remember that they found trusted leaders ready to sell the government for a price. But we are fooling ourselves if we believe a few fines and prison sentences have served to restore our national integrity.

Watergate isn't so very far from any of us, you see. Henry Steele Commager, the distinguished historian, made this point at a 1974 "Critical Issues Conference" of the National Education Association in Chicago. He said: *Did (not Mr. Nixon)—indeed, does he not—represent qualities in the American character that are widespread and even taken for granted? In himself and in the curious collection of associates he gathered around him, he represents the acquisitive society, the exploitative society, the aggrandizing society. He represents what is artificial, meretricious, and manipulative. He represents the American preference for the synthetic over the real, for advertising over the product, for public relations over character, for spectator sports over active games, and for spectator politics over participatory democracy. He represents, too, the widespread American conviction that anything can be bought: culture, education, happiness, a winning football team—or the Presidency.* [2]

If Watergate can become the occasion whereby we examine ourselves and seek integrity, not only in our political processes, but in the business and social life of our nation, then it may someday be looked upon as a blessing and not a curse. But it is entirely possible that we're now so tired of the details and removed by passing time from those events, that by the time we've seen the movies and read the books about *what* happened, we'll never get around to thinking seriously about *why* it happened. [3]

Some measure of the Watergate mentality is to be found in every unit of modern American society. The practice of deceit, the gathering of power, the suspending of rules, the philosophy of the end justifying the means, moral principles which are easily adjustable to suit the occasion, the corruption of language so that it becomes a tool of public relations instead of an instrument of truth—these are the practices of everyday. And it's unreasonable to expect that this can thrive in "Smithville, U.S.A.," and not come to Washington too.

The practice of taking short cuts, of suspending the rules to gain a personal advantage, is so widespread that it's difficult to find an area of our society which is not affected. It starts at the bottom and goes all the way to the top. It begins with shoplifting by supermarket customers—stealing one-half million shopping carts every year and adding 15 percent to the cost of every grocery item we buy—and it extends to price rigging by large supermarket chains.

College cheating is at an all-time high, we're told [4]—some of it on the very campuses where dishonesty in government draws a lot of attention by the very same students. One study placed the number of fraudulent insurance claims as high as 75 percent.

Whom can you trust to repair your car or television set or washing machine? When this time comes, aren't all of us suspicious of deceit; of parts charged for, but not replaced; of time charged for, but never spent? And yet, most people find ways to make up the deficit by doing the same thing to someone else, in other ways: They steal from their employer or cheat on their taxes.

The director of the IRS says the government loses at least five billion dollars annually through deliberately fraudulent tax returns. Claiming personal expenditures as legitimate business expense is said to be one of the most frequent.

In spite of recent legislation, some loan companies still disguise the actual cost of borrowing from the very persons least able to defend themselves against it.

The claims made by advertisers in this country are a striking example of how acceptable lying has become. Who really believes that toothpaste X will solve your dating problems, as the skit implies? That white-coated man who poses as a doctor and tells you to buy a certain product—who really believes he's for real? Does detergent A really get your clothes cleaner than brand B, like those demonstrations show? Who really believes those tire torture tests, and what about those advertised mileage figures which tell buyers that a car just like yours will give them twice the mileage yours is giving you?

We've gotten so used to these fabrications that they easily gain a quick acceptance. Then our President comes on the air and tells us, as he did April 17, 1973: "I condemn any attempts to cover up in this case, no matter who is involved." Later on, we find out that he told his closest associates just three weeks prior to this: "I want you all to stonewall it, let them plead the Fifth Amendment, cover up, or anything else." We can't say it's right; but we can't say we're surprised either, because we're used to looking *under* words to find out what the *real* truth is.

I found an insightful analysis of the Watergate mentality in a study by Bertram Raven of the University of California. He noted a kind of group dynamic which operated in the Nixon White House. There was pressure within the group to equal or exceed the zeal of others, and this runaway norm led to more extreme positions being taken—more risks, and more sacrifice of individual integrity. Raven said: "To be a rising member of the team you had to be loyal to the chief, steadfast, strong, hard-hitting, merciless to your enemies and not get wound up worrying about the methods which you used." [5] One of the best examples of this mentality is the saying of Charles Colson that he would walk over his grandmother if it became necessary! Surely we've seen by now the disastrous results of that mentality, but the question remains: will we learn from it and mend our ways?

Someone may perhaps be offended that I seem to suggest a kind of national guilt for Watergate. I would in no way excuse those directly responsible. They bear a special kind of guilt for betraying a special kind of trust. But if we do no more than blame and punish them, feeling justified in ourselves, we miss a great opportunity.

Every man who makes a deal, every person who takes an oath, every company which asks for loyalty, every workman who draws his pay, every reporter who tells the news—we all need a look at our own integrity through the prism of Watergate. The American nation still numbers some great and honorable persons, both men and women. But signs are abundant that it's high time for some honest reassessments, and perhaps some specific declarations:

If we have learned to tell the truth, even when it hurts or embarrasses;

If we have learned that our American dream script calls for democracy and not monarchy;

If we have learned that righteous living is a thousand times better than religious talking;

If we have learned that sin has a way of finding us out, even when we conceal it with great care.

If we have learned that it profits nothing to gain the whole world and lose our own soul;

Then our God, who must have looked upon us darkly in these past years, may show us again the smile of his approval.

# 8

## Improper Solutions

"When the days drew near for him to be received up, he set his face to go to Jerusalem. And he sent messengers ahead of him, who went and entered a village of the Samaritans, to make ready for him; but the people would not receive him, because his face was set toward Jerusalem. And when his disciples James and John saw it, they said, 'Lord, do you want us to bid fire come down from heaven and consume them?' But he turned and rebuked them," (Luke 9:51–55).

*I can't believe this! These people don't want us in their town, don't want us! Who do they think they are anyway? We're Jews, and they're just Samaritans. Most of our people wouldn't lower themselves to even come through this country, much less stop in one of their towns. But the Master was bound and determined to come by here. I wonder how he feels about it now? You know, he's always played up to these people. I suppose he feels sorry for them because they act so mistreated.*

*I didn't want to come through here in the first place. I just knew something like this would happen. This shows you can waste your time being too nice to people who don't appreciate it anyway. Oh, this makes me mad!*

*Listen, you thankless people, all this be-nice-to-one-another stuff is off—cancelled—and it's your own fault. From now on, as far as I'm concerned, it's all right back like it used to be. We stay in our place, and you stay in yours. You'd better stay in yours, because if you ever show your faces in our territory, there'll be bad trouble; do you hear?*

*Let me take care of this, Lord. I know what ought to be done, and I think I can handle it. Remember Sodom and Gomorrah and all that fire and brimstone? Remember how those Egyptians were drowned in the middle of the Red Sea? Remember how old Elijah called down fire on the prophets of Baal? That's what we need here—teach these people a lesson. Just say the word, Lord. Now! And we'll be done with it.*

What kind of solution was this? Jesus had extended a hand of friendship to an outcast race. He'd had it slapped, and the disciples were furious. Their first thought was to get even, to respond in kind, to call down fire from heaven.

What kind of solution was this? Didn't it represent the surrender of reason to the impulse of an angry moment? One of the first things we might learn here is never decide anything when you're angry and upset. And you can carry that a step further and recommend not saying very much either. The person who prides himself on bursting out with whatever he feels like saying, isn't going to help solve many problems. In fact, he will quickly become one himself. In the beginning, Jesus had just one problem: how to respond to the rejection of the Samaritans. Now, all of a sudden, there was another one: how to handle the anger of his own disciples, and discourage the solution they were urging so vigorously.

Call down fire from heaven! What kind of solution was this? Wasn't it the kind of quick, easy solution everyone dreams about, but seldom finds? Call in help from outside; get an expert to take care of it for us—isn't that a lot easier than getting personally involved? And isn't it ever so much easier to think of doing something *to* people than doing something *for* them or *with* them?

What kind of solution was this? Doesn't it reveal one of those embarrassing lapses, where suddenly all our high-sounding principles are forgotten, and we just hope God isn't looking, or someone doesn't catch us? After all, these men—James and John and the others—were disciples of the Golden Rule. They'd heard the Sermon on the Mount. They were in training to go out and preach good tidings of peace to all the nations! But here they were, proposing solutions you'd expect from generals or gangsters or ruthless investors—destroy the competition!

The Master expects more of his disciples than he does of others. He asked: "If all you do is just swap pleasantries with your friends, how are you any better than the crooks?" (see Matt. 5:47). And he added: "Just being religious isn't nearly enough. You've got to be a lot better than those scribes and Pharisees if you want to see the kingdom of heaven" (Matt. 5:20). So how dare we speak of calling down fire to punish people we don't even know, much less understand? Call that zeal if you like, but don't ever forget that it's possible to be zealous for the honor of God in a spirit which puts us out of fellowship with God.

You see, when we're beset with tough problems, we tend to forget that it still matters *how* we solve them. James and John wanted a sort of "miracle in reverse." They wanted God's power used to destroy and punish; and Jesus never, never did this. He always used his power to help and bless. Never once did he use it to take a life, or gain the upper hand, or settle a score.

Water he changed to wine; nets he filled with fish; fever he calmed; a widow's son he raised; five thousand he fed; ten lepers he restored; Lazarus he brought forth; a man born blind he gave sight; a storm he calmed; a man's severed ear he put back; a withered hand he made new and whole. How preposterous it is to think of the man who did those memorable works of kindness calling down fire to avenge a mere discourtesy. How sad that the men who proposed it were the very ones he counted on to show his spirit to others.

The temptation to work our miracles in reverse—to use our power for hurt instead of help—is still with us today. Do we take our nitrogen and put it in the soil to grow food for the hungry, or do we concoct deadly explosives with it? How do we use all our miracles of chemistry and electronics and biology and medicine? As a blessing, or a curse?

I know it's not as easy as that makes it sound. We do have problems—tough ones—but we'd better think long and hard about the solutions we propose. "Call down fire," said the disciples. "Go to another town," said Jesus. What a difference!

What does a prosperous country do with tough social problems like crime and poverty and alienation and disillusionment? Do we just call for stronger laws and more police, and watch the evening news behind locked doors to see what happens?

What does the church do in the face of rising demands for its services by those outside, and dwindling support of its efforts by those inside? Do we collapse in a spasm of blaming one another? Do we thrust our hands deep in a bag of cheap tricks, hoping one of them can save us? Do we lower our standards to make discipleship easier, changing the road signs around to make the broad way seem like the narrow way? Surely not. No matter what problems modern churches face, we must have integrity—integrity in membership, integrity in our message, integrity in the kind of spirit which can accept defeat in one village and move on to try again in another one.

Throughout our society, we see evidence of this need for integrity in the solutions we turn to. What does free enterprise do when the short-term good of the company is likely a long-term menace to people and their environment? What if your competition isn't going by the rules either? Who wants to make sacrifices when others don't?

From the inside of that dilemma, a selfish man will harbor the thought: "I'll get all I can out of this. Who cares what happens after that? I won't be around to live with it anyway, and the kids will just have to do the best they can."

From the outside, a thoughtful man will wonder if our society has the moral capacity to solve such problems. A college sophomore can see what must be done, but where is the leader who can get us to do it? We appear to be governed by our selfish greed, and we will not stand for leadership which talks about sacrifice.

What happens when these moments of choice come to you? How much does integrity count when the going gets rough? How do you determine the solutions to your own personal problems? How do you deal with those irritating people you find it so hard to get along with? Don't *you* feel like calling down fire sometimes?

I've seen that done. Two jealous partners in business; two women who both want to run the same club; two guys who both want the same girl; two pastors who don't get along; two drivers who both want the same lane; two students who both want to be head of the class—everywhere you go in life you find the potential for it. We strive, compare, and compete; we wear our nerves thin; we sell our souls for what others think about us.

Does it matter how you play that game? Isn't it good sense just to clobber the opposition any way you can, and be done with it? Sometimes it almost seems so. But remember, as you face these decisions, the counsel of Paul: "Be not overcome of evil, but overcome evil with good" (Rom. 12:21, KJV). Overcome evil with good, he says, *not with more evil.* And if we can search out how that applies to our dealing with others, we can know the difference between a proper solution and an improper one, between calling down fire and going to another village.

There are other times we face this problem. What do you do when your former sources of inspiration are attacked by dullness? Your marriage doesn't seem romantic like it used to; do you go running off, with a copy of *Playboy* in your hand, looking for someone more exciting? Is that a proper solution?

Your religion doesn't bring the joy it used to. Do you blame the church and quit? Do you join some passing parade that seems to offer more action? Or do you just turn your mind to other things,

74

and become a Sunday dropout? There are so many of those, you may never be missed! But is this really a proper solution to your quest for meaning in life and peace with God?

Perhaps you used to do a lot of service for others, but you got a little tired in that, or maybe there were some problems. Perhaps it seemed that no one really appreciated what you did. What's the solution to that? Do you withdraw and try to find refuge feeling sorry for yourself? Or do you go back, get involved, and forget yourself?

Where do you go when a happy abundance begins to look like a miserable shortage, and something starts inside you which almost has to be called fear? All kinds of solutions present themselves in a time like that. And in the years ahead, we may have many opportunities to observe the response of people to the challenge of hardship. And the solutions to which we turn will declare what kind of moral stuff we're made of.

Fighting one another—we could easily fall into that. A national policy of turning away from world need—we could adopt that. Some kind of revolution, where the masses seize wealth by force—we could try that. Someone recently stated that we could balance the national budget if we legalized gambling and prostitution—we could turn to those. And, on a personal level, there are endless ways a man may take a shortcut, if the principle doesn't matter.

But the principle matters; that's the point. It matters for a man who believes in God who made us, and gave us commandments to live by. It matters for a man who wants to preserve something for his children. It matters for a man who looks to the future, knowing that no matter how tough the issue seems, panic can only make it worse. It matters for a man who values above all his other valuables, his own self-respect.

Jesus didn't accept the disciples' solution. Sure, it was hard to turn away from that village. It was sad to know that a worthy offer of friendship had been refused. For a person who loved the

Samaritans, and wanted to help, there was pain in it. *It was the pain of a proper solution.*

*We'll just go on now. We'll have to leave them alone for now. But we'll not be angry or vengeful. Remember when I said to repay no man evil for evil, but instead to bless? Remember when I said to go the second mile if someone compels you to go the first? Remember I told you we're not to say "an eye for an eye" any more? So come on, and shame on you all for thinking of revenge. Think of help; there'll be another day to help.*

Because of that spirit, that determination to resist improper solutions, we read from the record of John's gospel about another, happier day in Samaria: *Many Samaritans from that city believed in him because of the woman's testimony . . . So when the Samaritans came to him, they asked him to stay with them; and he stayed there two days. And many more believed because of his word. They said to the woman, "It is no longer because of your words that we believe, . . . and we know that this is indeed the Savior of the world"* (John 4:39–42).

# 9

## In God We Are Trustworthy

*In God we trust*—this is the proclamation of every coin that jingles in our pockets. And that's fine; we need trust and faith—the man-to-God dimension of life. But there's another angle to this trust which seems especially urgent in the post-Watergate era. Can it also be said that *in God we are trustworthy?* Has your trust in God made you trustworthy to others? Can fellow members of your society depend on your integrity; or must they watch you, keep files on you, secure their property around you, build defenses toward you, and fear what might happen if some day you should gain the upper hand?

Even in the Old Testament, this need for trustworthiness was recognized. *You shall not pervert justice*, the Lord says in Deuteronomy. *You shall not show partiality; and you shall not take a bribe, for a bribe blinds the eyes of the wise and subverts the cause of the righteous. Justice, and only justice, you shall follow, that you may live and inherit the land which the Lord your God gives you* (Deut. 16:19–20). And the message of those words is plain: in God a man is trustworthy.

We wouldn't ordinarily think of John the Baptist as a preacher of the social gospel. He comes across more along the lines of a fundamentalist-type evangelist. And yet one afternoon John had some penetrating advice, which speaks straight at the issue of our trustworthiness in society. Many were coming to be baptized by him in the river Jordan. The Gospel of Luke then tells us: *Tax collectors also came to be baptized, and said to him, "Teacher,*

77

*what shall we do?"* At that point, you'd almost certainly expect some plainly *religious* answer—something like "believe in God," or "trust in God," or "receive the Messiah who is to come." But instead of this, John spoke about integrity in the world of business: *He said to them, "Collect no more than is appointed you!"* And right after that, a similar thing happened: *Soldiers also asked him, "And we, what shall we do?" And he said to them, "Rob no one by violence or by false accusation, and be content with your wages!"* (Luke 3:12–14).

When men ask directions today, when they stand in the hallways of the church, saying "What shall we do?" it's well to answer "Trust in God." But we must go on, as John did, to add: ". . . and in him, be trustworthy toward others." Whether the man is a tax collector or a soldier or any one of a thousand other vocations, unheard of in those simpler days, he will find a momentous task of deciding what it means to live his kind of life, and be trustworthy.

Later on in the New Testament, the apostle Paul spoke of what it meant for him. He said: *We have renounced disgraceful, underhanded ways; we refuse to practice cunning or to tamper with God's word, but by the open statement of the truth we would commend ourselves to every man's conscience in the sight of God* (2 Cor. 4:2). And the message is clear: in God we are trustworthy.

Brooks Hays, the former Arkansas congressman, once told about a man who was called as witness in an election bribery case. He finally admitted that he took ten dollars to vote Democratic. Then, it came out that he'd also taken ten dollars to vote Republican! And when they asked him how he had actually voted, he replied that he'd just voted his conscience!

Rumor tells about a treaty signed with the Indians which provided that they would have their lands as long as the sun shone, the river flowed, and the rain fell to earth. But at the bottom of the page, in small print, it said: "Or within ninety days, whichever comes first!"

But, to speak of the issue more seriously, I have a feeling that the crisis of America in the mid-seventies is something like that of Germany in the mid-forties. When the bombs finally stopped falling on Berlin, the German people found the need to adjust to two grim realities: they had lost a war, and they had been witness to terrible crimes by their trusted leaders. They had lost their war in spite of tremendous sacrifice, patriotism, and occasional brilliance. But when the full story of the war crimes and death marches and extermination camps was told, a decent man must have found himself wondering what was left to build the future with.

With the fall of American-supported South Vietnam, and the final humiliation of all our military efforts there, and with the Watergate scandal fully exposed, doesn't America have something of the same task? Sure, a man may protest that *he* had nothing to do with it, that it was all the fault of others. But for those who think honestly, questions will keep coming. Maybe we were guilty too; maybe we *let* it happen, or didn't *care* that much about it. Maybe we might have done the same thing, or as someone said to me: "Politics is a dirty business. I don't blame them. They were just unlucky enough to get caught at it."

I believe we must admit that some national failures took place for which all Americans must accept a measure of responsibility. Were it not for the economic recession of 1975, followed by political speechmaking for the elections of 1976, perhaps we could and would have given proper thought and reflection to these sobering issues—as the Germans seem to have given to theirs. The times demand a national repentance, and a ruthless thoroughgoing effort to restore trustworthiness in all the basic structures of our society. One of the greatest present weaknesses of our country is not that we lack planes and guns, but that we lack a basic element of trust in our country's leadership at all levels. And here I use the term *weakness* in precisely the same sense it is often used by the Pentagon and the American Legion.

These are hard times for would-be leaders of all varieties. Just think of the people we depend upon the most, and you have a list of those we trust the least: mayors of cities, chiefs of police, school superintendents, labor union leaders, hospital supervisors, utility board chairmen, newspaper editors, television news commentators, clergymen, university professors, military generals, physicians, attorneys, state legislators, senators, supreme court justices, presidents. Isn't there a general feeling that somehow these people have let us down, that we can't expect them to do anything for us, that they're all out for themselves, that they're just not doing the job we pay them for? And when society becomes polarized into competing enclaves of self-interest, which look at every issue in terms of their own advantage or disadvantage—who *wants* to sit in the chair where decisions have to be made for the good of *all* the people?

There has to be trust or we will wrangle ourselves into national exhaustion. And before there can be trust, there must be trustworthiness in the trustee; and there must be respect and goodwill in the truster; and perhaps most important, there must be a flow of honest and open communication between the two, so that they perceive each other as friends, not as adversaries.

We must trust our President and Congress to tell us the truth, and to serve the nation instead of themselves. We must trust our police and law-enforcement agencies to resist corruption by those who would make them a tool of self-interest and oppression. We must trust our educational systems to teach the values we cherish. We must trust our news media to report events with integrity. We must trust our judicial system to be truly fair. We must trust our large and powerful corporations to have a social conscience. We must trust our vast military establishment to join us in seeking world peace.

In big things, and in little things, we depend on the trustworthiness of others. And the more interrelated and complex our society becomes, the more acute becomes the need for it. Let me give a timely example: If I should be suddenly killed in an accident, I'd be most happy for any salvaged part of my body to be used for the benefit of the living. You may have said the same thing yourself. But what if you make this agreement and someone, knowing it, doesn't make the utmost effort to save your life? It might seem a slim hope anyway, so he just goes ahead and grabs out your heart and kidneys or whatever else he can use. Is that preposterous? No one would do that, you say? I hope not; but do you see how we depend on the trustworthiness of others, and how they depend on us?

I think it would be well for all elections in this country to be publicly financed, and do away with people buying influence through campaign contributions. But what if we all agree to this idea, and give our part by checking some appropriate space on form 1040? Can we trust those who distribute millions of our dollars to do it fairly? And can we trust those running for office to play it by the rules?

It all comes down to *people*. People make the difference. And no matter how we may perfect the system—embellish it with wisdom, fence it with safeguards, warn those who would abuse it, and promise reward to those who maintain it—it can still be no better than the personal integrity of the people who are a part of it.

Because of this, the trustworthiness we seek won't come to pass solely through enactment of legislation in Congress. You can't legislate morality, or for that matter, honesty, or trust, or integrity. Nor will it come to pass solely through getting the right man for President of the country. We expect too much when we dream of one man in the White House changing our whole population. Nor will it come to pass solely through a system of economic incentives for men to be good. History has never shown us that a man can get rich enough to stop cheating in order to get richer. Nor will it come to pass solely through the toughness of judges or juries or police or detectives or guards or investigators. Someone will always be trying to prove he's tougher.

The only solution is a religious solution. It was none other than George Washington who said: "Reason and experience both forbid us to expect that national morality can prevail in exclusion of religious principle." [6] Henry Ward Beecher, who served the pulpit of Brooklyn's Plymouth Congregational Church for almost half the nineteenth century, once stated the same thing in a sermon. He said there "is no true and abiding morality that is not founded in religion." [7]

I hold it to be one of history's lessons, that in God, and in God alone, is a man made trustworthy. In God we are trustworthy; but apart from God we will never be trustworthy. I mean this in no narrow, sectarian way. I'm not saying you have to be a Methodist or a Catholic or a Baptist or a Jew. I'm not even saying you have to be part of any organized religious group, though I encourage it. I'm simply suggesting that religious faith is the place to begin—that religious man, converted man, is the man we need.

Perhaps it would help if I describe such a man: *He knows himself to be accountable to One who is eternal and omnipotent. He believes in him as one who sees all he does, hears all he says, knows his very thoughts, and* cares.

*He knows that there are moral laws which cannot be excused on demands of expediency: "Thou shalt not kill; thou shalt not steal; thou shalt not covet; thou shalt not commit adultery; thou shalt not bear false witness; honor thy father and thy mother." "Repay no man evil for evil." "As you would that men should do to you, do ye even so to them." "Love thy neighbor as thyself . . . ." Religious man will always fail to be a perfect keeper of those laws, but he will never fail to be conscious of them, especially as he breaks them.*

*He prays for guidance; he earnestly searches for help and direction. In his decidings, he answers to an* oughtness, *which he knows to be the voice of God himself, however faint and however confusing.*

*Religious man will actually deny himself of that which self-interest proposes, and do it for the sake of his integrity.*

*He lives in fellowship with others of like mind, who help him in his struggle. With them he confesses his failings, and to them he turns again and again for strength and affirmation.*

It used to be thought that a few such men as leaders could ensure the health of our society. It must surely now be apparent that the need is greater—much greater—and that, in fact, nothing less than the unlikely abundance of such persons can ensure our survival.

# Part IV

## Integrity as an Inner Honesty

Dear Conscience:

Isn't there ever to be any peace between us? You'd think that after all these years of pain and pulling, one of us would get tired, and just give in.

Other people don't seem to have all the problems we do. Why, I just read an article by a smart man who wants to solve the hunger problem by letting half the world starve to death. And he described it with all the ease of a comedian giving a familiar routine.

Why can't it be that way with us? Why do I have to be so moral about everything that comes up? Why do I have to worry over the rightness or wrongness of things others take for granted? Am I really that good, or do I just enjoy the suffering?

# 10

## The Anatomy of Hypocrisy

The scene is Antioch, center of the Gentile-Christian world in that crucial first century. Antioch—where Paul started each of his three great missionary journeys. Antioch—where John Chrysostom, one of the greatest early spokesmen for the Christian faith, began his ministry. Antioch—where a liberalizing, cosmopolitan spirit gathered momentum to collide with, and eventually overcome, the narrowness of a faith still tied to the apron strings of Judaism.

It was supper time, and the church of Antioch gathered to break bread. This was usually an hour of shared gladness and thanksgiving, but tonight there was strain in the air. There were grim looks, and little circles of whispering, and hurried glances around the room.

Company had come. Paul, the great missionary hero, was there. Barnabas, his trusted friend, was there. Simon Peter was there. Yes, Simon. They had worried about him at first. What would he think of a church where Jews and Gentiles sat down as brothers together, where circumcision was forgotten and the old Jewish food laws broken at every meal?

It had gone well at first. Peter had stepped into an atmosphere he'd never known in Jerusalem, but he handled it well. On a rooftop in Joppa, God had dramatically illustrated to him that all men are brothers (Acts 10). Now, for the first time, he saw it in operation—a living fellowship of persons, both Jews and Gentiles. For a few brief days, he had been a part of it, shared it, felt it, wondered at it, admired it, and thanked God for it.

But then other faces had appeared: men from Jerusalem, stern Jewish men, men who would report on Peter's actions when they returned, men who didn't eat with Gentiles, men who didn't understand. Now, suddenly, it wasn't as easy as it had seemed. Now, all at once, there was a choice to make. Oh, how Peter wished he could just be excused and avoid that choice, but there was no way.

The sweet fellowship which used to fill their room was soured. The strangers from Jerusalem sat by themselves. Peter sat with them. Barnabas sat with them. Some Jewish members of the Antioch church also withdrew from their brothers, and sat with them. Their frail alliance, their holy experiment, was crushed like a paper cup under a heavy boot. Or at least it seemed that way to a Jew from Tarsus, who still sat with his Gentile friends, burning inside, and wondering if he should try to keep in his rage or just let it come out.

*Peter, you hypocrite! Playactor, pretender—don't you see what you've done now? I know I'm supposed to be respectful of you, because you traveled with Christ and I didn't. But how can I respect what you've done here? How could Christ be pleased with it?*

*You ate with us. And you know that Jews and Gentiles are all the same with God. Then these stooges come from James, and you act like you've been kosher all along. Well it won't work, because I'm going to tell them! I'm going to tell them right here in this room, in front of all these people. Maybe when you've been exposed, when there's no place to hide, you'll be free to choose the way that's right instead of acting out this farce.*

He did it, just like that. Paul rebuked Peter to his face, and the brotherhood was tested. But the church survived, and Paul survived, and Peter survived. And years later Peter may have remembered that night when he wrote in one of his letters: "Laying aside all . . . hypocrisies" (1 Pet. 2:1, KJV). (Also, for the New

Testament account of this story, see Gal. 2:11–16.)

If we're going to be men and women of integrity, we've got to deal with that subtlety which allows us to change convictions as often as we change companions. What must we do with this falseness which gives us leave to teach one thing and live another? This arrogance to make high-sounding claims for no other purpose than deception? This game we play by hiding our true selves while we try to peddle another one?

*Hey there people, things are really great with this old boy! Never felt better in my life. Work hard every day, you can believe that. None of this handout stuff for me! What I've got I've earned, and you can believe that. Made it honest, too. Ask anyone, they'll tell you. Got a beautiful wife, a happy home, lovely children. Hey, see that car of mine? Beauty, isn't it? Runs great, too. Drove it all the way to Texas to see an old buddy of mine last summer. Got a lot of friends; friends all over the country. Well, got to be going now. Say, if you ever need anything, you know who to see.*

As the car door slams, it ends the monologue on a note of solid luxury. And as Mr. America pulls away and flicks on the car stereo, you're almost tempted to believe all that stuff. Don't do it. Behind that mask is a person who has the same fears you do, the same loneliness you do, the same frustration that life isn't working out as planned, the same guilt over breaking the rules, the same worries about his health, the same struggle to get along at home, the same need to be accepted and approved by others. His expensive, new suit may help a little, but it doesn't change that.

The essence of hypocrisy is to conceal one's real character— one's real purposes—under the mask of something different. And Mr. America has perfected that art.

One day some people came to Jesus with a coin of the Roman government. *Master, we just want to know something. Just a question for our own help and benefit. We're not trying to trick you or anything like that. Just between us now, just an honest*

91

*question now, is it right to pay taxes to Rome or not?* But the Bible says that Jesus knew their hypocrisy (Mark 12:13–16, KJV). He answered the question, but he wasn't fooled by the game they were playing. He may have even struggled to conceal his amusement. And very shortly afterward, he brought home the lesson to his disciples: *Beware of the leaven of the Pharisees, which is hypocrisy. Nothing is covered up that will not be revealed, or hidden that will not be known. Whatever you have said in the dark shall be heard in the light, and what you have whispered in private rooms shall be proclaimed upon the housetops* (Luke 12:1–2).

I thought of that verse as I drove down Virginia Avenue between the Watergate and Howard Johnson's, where the listening went on. I thought about it when Butterfield told the Senate committee about the listening devices installed in the White House. Soon afterward, we learned about other listening going on: listening in people's offices, listening to people's mail, listening to private phone conversations. And we must banish that kind of illegal spying from our land if we possibly can. But there's another point to make—one which claims that the God who made us not only listens to what we say, but knows our thoughts as we say them. And he's the only one who really matters in the long run of things. So why this cover-up with everyone else?

Matthew's Gospel gives an interesting case. The subject is a man who ought to spend money to help his aging parents, but he's too selfish for that. Does he say: "Sorry Mom and Dad. You raised a stingy boy, and I'm not willing to help you"? No, of course not. He says: "I'd really like to help. I would if I could. But, you see, I made a vow to God. I've dedicated my property to him. And I can't break that vow to God. I'm *so* sorry." (See Matt. 15:4–9.) And Jesus, who knew men's hearts and loved an honest one, called that hypocrisy.

Sometimes our deceiving works. Sometimes we fool the whole world and feel secure. Sometimes we fool some, while others know us better. Sometimes a man deceives no one, but still he plays the part and says the words, while everyone listens and smiles. King Herod, who wanted that young Jesus-child dead, because they sang about his being a king someday—that same Herod said to three stargazers from the East: "When you have found him, bring me word, that I too may come and worship him" (Matt. 2:8). Would anyone who believes that, please stand up? The king would like it, but even the boy who scrubs the harness leather knows better than that.

Human nature is so very subtle. We think one thing, but we say another. We say it, and try to sell it; because if we can sell it to someone else, we may convince ourselves it's worth something after all.

In *The Nature and Destiny of Man*, Reinhold Niebuhr described it this way: "If others will only accept what the self cannot quite accept, the self as deceiver is given an ally against the self as deceived." [1]

Two young men grew up together in a small farming community. One had gone to school, learned a trade, worked hard, built a nice home, and gained the respect of his elders. The other had taken odd jobs—just enough to get money for shotgun shells, old cars, bird dogs, and some fun in town now and then. He finally got married and lived in a shack. He drove an old car you could hear a mile away. Now there was nothing wrong with all that, of course. It was just that he would often tell me he didn't care about nice homes and new cars and fancy clothes like his friend had. He told me that *so many times*, I knew it was just the opposite. Inside he wanted all those things, and felt guilty that he'd trifled his time away when he could have earned them.

Watch out for the man who tells you he cares nothing about money; he'll cheat you. Watch out for the man who says he never told a lie; you're about to be taken in. Watch out for the man who says too often that he loves everybody; he's about to hurt someone.

Unless the light of God and the truth of God can be our constant companions, we will spend out lives deceiving and deceived. We'll fail to get honest answers from honest questions. We'll take an awfully long time to find out if we can trust someone, and then not be sure. Everything we hear, we'll have to question—*Am I being informed with truth or manipulated with lies? What's the hidden agenda here? What are they up to now?*

I think we must also face the fact that hypocrisy goes to church, just as it goes to the office, the market, the beauty shop, the Congress, and all those other fun places. In fact, the skeptic will describe the church as hypocrisy organized—people acting pious on Sunday, and worldly through the week; ministers playing God; members doing things to get recognition, and having their feelings hurt if they don't receive it; everything nice and clean, just like God wants it—no smoking; no drinking; no cussing; no dirty clothes (wear your "Sunday best"); no loud talking, please; no dirty jokes (tell me when we get outside!).

The skeptic is partly right in what he observes, but he's wrong in believing the church is the only place where this hypocrisy thrives, or that it's the worst. Church is also the place where people are trying to get free from ghettos of too-small moralities. And one discovers a significant number who are sincerely trying to be natural before God, and natural with others—to become both real and Christian at the same time.

I have my own testimony here. The minister, of all people, is haunted with the question: "What do they think of me? How did I do this morning? Do I seem good enough?"

My own ministerial pilgrimage began with a need to be very conservative, because that's what was expected. I can recall preaching on hell a lot (that was the most conservative subject I could think of!). And when I would say the word, I'd say it loud and with stern authority—hell!

Then later other influences entered my life, and there was a need to prove myself educated and liberal. So I would bravely attack the King James Version, or speak on the race issue, or refer to a technical Greek word I'd only learned the night before.

Maybe we all have to go through stages like that—stages when we need acceptance by a group—and we pretend a bit to get it. But our goal must be freedom—freedom to be ourselves, to be honest, to take no man's party line, to march to our own drummer, to be the original and not the carbon, to say "I think" instead of "me too." If someone calls that conservative, that's his business. If he calls it liberal, let him be happy or mad as the case may be. Let the *I* come out, because it's all you have to give to the world. And if you bury it or hide it or doctor it up or welsh on it, you'll be sorry when life is almost gone and the *I* never really lived.

The real *you* is worth giving: your thoughts, your fears, your joys, your hopes, and dreams. You don't have to redecorate it or muffle it or gag it. And when you give it—the real *you*, without hypocrisy, without pretense—you feel something come surging back which deserves to live, something like health or wonder or excitement.

We began with the church at Antioch, with a man caught in the grip of pressure to conform. We saw him yield to that pressure, play a part, and become a spectacle of pretense. If we've the wisdom to learn from that story, it might take the form of repealing the premium we place on hypocrisy and the grudging respect we give to those, like Mr. America, who practice it.

Let's give one another the freedom to let the *I* come out. Let's go by the spirit of the law, which gives life, and not by the letter of the law, which encourages deceit. Let's not abuse this thing called recognition, so that we scramble for it and fight one another for it and pretend goodness in order to get it. Let's place no premium at all on religious talk. Not every one that saith "Lord, Lord" shall enter the Kingdom, but he who does the will of the Father, and does it in spirit and in truth.

The Father seeketh such to worship him.

# 11

## My Faith in Doubt

It seems fair to say that the word *doubt* has a very questionable reputation, at least around churches. There is a mildly subversive ring to it, as if all we've worked for might suddenly be destroyed if much of it gets in.

You're supposed to bring your faith when you come to church, not your doubt. The Sunday crowds want to hear a sermon filled with strong faith, not with shrinking doubts. "Give me the benefit of your convictions," said Goethe, the great German poet, "but keep your doubts to yourself, for I have enough of my own." [2] Someone else wrote that doubt digs the grave of faith, and Sir Walter Scott, who admired Goethe, expressed it in these strong terms: "Better had they ne'er been born, who read to doubt, or read to scorn." [3]

According to Kathryn Rogers Deering, a contemporary writer: "Doubts are the greasy fingerprints on your camera lens . . . the gravy stains on your new white tablecloth . . . the mold on that piece of bread which has been left too long in your cupboard . . . the keys of your piano with the ivory knocked off . . . the bent dimes which clog up your Coke machine." [4]

Most people suppose that when you come to church you should come with a Bible in your hand, an offering in your pocket, a smile on your clean-scrubbed face, and your halo on straight. If you have doubts, at least have the decency to keep them to yourself.

I have another view: a view that honest doubt is honorable;

that it is supportive to faith, not subversive; that we ought to bring it to church; and that, in some sense, the achievement of integrity awaits a rediscovery of the value of doubt.

We seem to be a lot like Justice Hitz, who presided over the Federal Appeals Court of Washington. One day he leaned over the bench and said to a protesting lawyer: "My friend, this court is often in error, but never in doubt." [5]

"Often in error, but never in doubt." Does that describe the church? Does it describe our personal approach to God? If it does, couldn't it be that *if we were more often in doubt, we might be less often in error?* We assume that doubt is a substance which stains us, but, in fact, it may be the very substance we need to cleanse us.

Robert Browning suggested this in a poem titled "Bishop Blougram's Apology": "You call for faith: I show you doubt, to prove that faith exists. The more of doubt, the stronger faith, I say, if faith o'ercomes doubt." [6]

René Descartes, the seventeenth-century French philosopher, went so far as to contend: "If you would be a real seeker after truth, it is necessary that at least once in your life you doubt, as far as possible, all things." [7] Descartes sought to reform philosophy by applying this radical doubt to all existing ideas. As a result, he arrived at a basic affirmation: *Cogito, ergo sum*; "I think, therefore I am." This, he said, you cannot doubt. From this, Descartes turned to the first distinctive idea a thinking man is aware of: God, the all good, all wise, and all powerful. This was the foundation of his philosophy, and it began with doubt.

In the Bible, and in Christian history, great believers have often been great doubters. Jesus never praised a man more highly than John the Baptist—that strong man who had declared him Lamb of God, who had baptized him in Jordan, who had said "I'm not worthy to untie his shoes." But after all this, from the deepening gloom of a prison cell, John sends the man from Nazareth a tormented question: "Are you he who is to come, or shall we look for another?" (Luke 7:20).

*It's cold and miserable in this jail. The crowds that used to follow me are with you now. Why have I been here so long? Why haven't you come to get me out? What's going to happen to me before it's over? Could it all have been a great mistake? Surely not; I've worked so long and hard for it. But just once more, before I die, let me hear it from you "Lamb of God"—tell me it's really so.*

Everything depended on that, you see. Jesus was Messiah, or Messiah had not come. There was no alternative, no middle ground. Either God through Christ has saved us, or we're lost; either the soul survives at death, or it doesn't; either man is made in God's image, or we count no more than insects flying about; either there's a moral foundation to the universe, or nothing makes sense at all. Most of the big questions are like John's. They leave us no middle ground of neutrality, and even when we've answered them time and time again, they have a way of coming back to stare at us once more.

One of the twelve had a way of raising questions like those. Sometimes we even hear him referred to as "Doubting Thomas." John's Gospel tells us the most about Thomas. When Jesus set himself on going to Jerusalem—leaving safe territory and inviting opposition—it was Thomas who said: "Let us also go, that we may die with him" (John 11:16). There's not a lot of hope in that determined statement, but a lot of courage, and a lot of commitment.

And do you remember the honest doubt this man expressed when Jesus spoke of going away to heaven? "You know the way," Jesus had said. But Thomas alone had the honesty to confess: "We do not know; I'm sorry. Please tell us" (see John 14:5).

But the summit of Thomas' pilgrimage to faith was at one of Christ's appearances after his resurrection. Thomas had been absent the first time the disciples saw him. They had told him about it, but he couldn't believe it from them. He'd have to see for himself, he said. No rumor carried, no story heard and passed on for what it was worth—firsthand evidence, that's what Thomas wanted. He wanted to see with his own eyes, handle with his own hands, and prove in his own experience the reality of what these men were telling. Even their obvious excitement wasn't enough for him.

He got his chance—the risen Jesus standing there saying: "Put your finger here, and see my hands; and put out your hand, and place it in my side; do not be faithless, but believing. And Thomas answered: 'My Lord, and my God' " (John 20:27–28).

Having satisfied his doubt, having secured the experience firsthand, having guaranteed the integrity of his belief—Thomas pronounced one of the loftiest confessions of faith in all Christian history. And in that moment, he was the world's most eloquent spokesman for the truth he had so recently struggled to accept.

We think of Paul as a man of strong faith. We hear him say that "nothing in all the world can separate us from Christ's love . . . tribulation, or distress, or persecution" (see Rom. 8:35). But this very same man also wrote: "We were so utterly, unbearably crushed that we despaired of life itself" (2 Cor. 1:8).

Someone run quick and throw a sheet over that, so we don't have to look it in the face! Let's not read about Paul's doubt; let's read about his faith—that's what people want. But don't you think it's important, if the time comes when *you* feel unbearably crushed, to know you're not the first, and that it's no sign God has cast you aside?

Martin Luther certainly had a strong faith. He wrote: "A mighty fortress is our God,/ A bulwark never failing. Our helper he, amid the flood/ Of mortal ills prevailing." But shouldn't we also be told that he was once so despondent his wife dressed herself in mourning clothes and said she was mourning the death of God. From the way Luther was behaving, she declared, God must surely be dead!

Can't we find the same thing in Job's experience? He doubted

God and questioned him and complained to him. But why was it God preferred his faith to the orthodoxy of those three friends? Could it be there was more faith in Job's questions than in all their pious answers?

What about that garden called Gethsemane? Faith was expressed there, certainly. But wasn't faith won at the cost of doubt and struggle? Jesus doubting—is that heresy? If so, then how on earth can we interpret his tormented question: "My God, My God, why hast thou forsaken me?" (Mark 15:34).

A question like his is one we come back to as we encounter what the psalmist did: "Why are you cast down, O my soul, and why are you disquieted within me?" (Ps. 42:5). Some days everything seems right. Some days we want to cry out to the Lord that even the demons are subject to us. But the hour of doubting comes, and we cry out our fear and frustration, saying: "Carest thou not that we perish?" (Mark 4:38, KJV). And if someone tells us then, "You mustn't say that," how miserable we will be.

I'd like to assure you that doubt is a normal part of a growing, Christian experience. It may just indicate that you're moving from a secondhand faith to a firsthand faith, from accepting what you've heard to really knowing what you believe. Doubt also has something to do with moods. John the Baptist, lonely in that prison; Paul, exhausted from his labors—even when there aren't reasons as clear as those, let's remember that all faith has its high and lows. And if we're wise, we learn from both, and find God in both.

You can say this about doubt: it shows a person has been thinking, and that, in itself, is good for something. John Calvin said once that there was a "shameless fellow" who asked a pious man what God had done before the creation of the world. And the dear saint countered that he'd been "building hell for the curious." But in defense of the skeptic, let me say that there can be more faith in some people's doubt than in others' certainties. And just possibly there is also a hell for the gullible!

In telling the positive values of doubt, I'm not suggesting you go around saying "I doubt that" to everything you hear. And if you can honestly live in constant faith, without raising questions and struggling with doubts, then blessings on you. But whether the experience turns out to be mild or traumatic, each of us needs to bring an element of scrutiny to his religious life.

The cause of integrity is served by such scrutiny. All of us are good at judging others, but the greater value lies in judging ourselves—doubting, probing, questioning. And most of the time, when a man does that, it gives assurance of his sincerity. *The honest doubter is always sincere.* And in this age where deception is so widespread, that's important. "How can we find an honest man?" Look for one who can honestly express his doubts.

At a national conference I attended, the topic was the integrity of the denomination. The panelists were a mixed lot: a denominational executive, a prominent pastor-antagonist, and a religious journalist. I must somewhat oversimplify to make the point, but as I heard these men, this is what they seemed to be saying: The executive's position was that the denomination had integrity, and he was sure of it. The pastor's position was that the denomination lacked integrity, and he was sure of that. The editor was somewhere in between, but in a curious way.

He described the difficulties of maintaining integrity in a world of pressures to conform. He admitted errors of his own in dealing with those pressures. He seemed to be a man thinking out loud about problems he'd faced—ones he still had doubts about—and I found comfort in his doubting. Does that sound crazy? You doubt a man who says he believes; you believe a man who says he doubts. The man who seems sure of everything, who seems never to have doubted anything, may have a dishonest belief—a belief come secondhand, or adopted for convenience or for advantage. But when a man gives evidence of the struggle of conscience, the encounter with doubt, and the search for honest truth, you more readily trust the integrity of what he says.

I have faith in doubt. Not by itself, of course, but when it's one of God's ways to strengthen, establish, and settle us; when it helps us be ready to give answer to any man who asks a reason for the hope that is within us; and when it gives us the freedom to confess our faith, while admitting its failures and seeking its improvement—then it is our friend, and God's.

The distressed father of a boy in trouble said it best and most simply. Mark's Gospel tells the story. The son was terribly afflicted, and Jesus said: *Man, your boy can be well if you have faith enough. Do you? Do you really believe?* And that anxious seeker uttered the whole paradox of faith and doubt when he cried out: *Lord, I believe. Help my unbelief* (Mark 9:24).

I feel sorry for the man who says: "Lord, I don't believe and don't intend to." Even God can't help that man. And I feel just as sorry for the man who says: "Lord, I believe, and I'm perfectly satisfied with my belief." That man, too, has put himself beyond God's reach. But a faith that can affirm itself, express its honest doubt, and reach out for strength—that faith lives.

*Lord, I believe; help thou my unbelief.*

*Lord, I am pure in heart; cleanse thou my impurity.*

*Lord, I'm not ashamed to bear testimony of thee to others; help thou my fear of testimony.*

*Lord, I'm motivated only by a love for you and my fellowmen; help thou my vain and jealous thoughts, my prideful ways, and the dreadful selfishness I can never escape.*

*Lord, I'm not afraid to die; help thou my fear of death.*

*Lord, I'll follow you wherever you lead; help thou my unfollowing, and my half-following, and after all my mis-following, lead me home to be with thee.*

# 12

## The Quest for a Good Conscience

At least thirty times the New Testament makes direct reference to a person's conscience. The majority of these references are from the writings of one man—a man whose life had seen great extremes; a man who had abandoned a promising career with the majority religion to be a member of a despised minority sect; a man who would always remember his part in the jailing and torturing and killing of innocent people; a man who sought to work out the meaning of Christian morality in the context of encounter with every religious and pagan culture known to his day.

The life and thought of this man Paul may be considered as the quest for a good conscience. And I think this may be true of most great lives. It was certainly true of Augustine and Luther and Roger Williams. It stands out boldly in the struggles of Jefferson and Madison, Payne and Washington.

And today, as we seek moral directions in the post-Watergate era, it must become a national struggle. For haven't we all emerged from this ordeal hungry for leadership we can trust, leadership with integrity, leadership which tells the truth, leadership which may even lay aside the urges of expediency for the sake of conscience? In addition, haven't we begun to suspect that the rest of us may not be so pure and upright either, that the voice of an earnest conscience may be missing from the business world, and the medical world, and the legal world, and the taxpayer's world, and the military world, and all the other little worlds where people seek their fortunes?

Leon Jaworski, the former Watergate Special Prosecutor, was quoted in a subsequent article commenting on the lessons of Watergate. He said: "There's a great lesson in this. You'd better adhere to the right, and not start going toward the wrong. Because you're bound to take that extra step. It's like that German nurse at Hadamar. When she started out it was maybe only euthanasia, but pretty soon she was beginning to fudge, and then it was a lot easier just to kill anybody who came along. The principle's the same. I have no doubt that Nixon didn't start out with any such ideas of eventual wrongdoing. But then time went by, he got callous, and there was a laxity about following up on people not being truthful. So that when things got pretty darn difficult, he was cut off from everything, and devoting so much time to trying to undo wrongdoing, that that's what broke him." [8]

There are at least three alternatives with regard to a man's conscience. It's certainly true that some people seem to have none at all—no voice to commend for doing well, or condemn for doing ill—just a silence, a nothing, an indifference to any moral concern.

At the other end of the spectrum, there's the conscience which always disturbs, troubles, and chastens. But here, at least, there is potential for improvement. There's no certainty that a guilty man will ever change, but there's an absolute certainty that without this moral remorse, nothing can improve.

A pastor wrote of a woman who used to sometimes attend his small congregation, much to the dismay of the regular worshipers. You see, her reputation was a scandal—she was a prostitute—and people wished she would just stay away. But she came, the pastor says, and sometimes took communion. Other times she passed it on, and just sat quietly weeping. Guilty she was, but at least there is hope in a bad conscience like that. The pastor even thought she was closer to God than some of those who just assumed their goodness without any such struggle.

104

Our goal, of course, is in the direction of the remaining alternative—a good conscience. It is not the assurance of perfection, but the satisfaction of being true to our ideals. It is not a record of having been always right, but the integrity of having done what we thought was right.

Now conscience isn't a static thing; it ought to change with times that change and people who grow in understanding and faith. If you've been on the journey of life for very long, you know yours has changed. There are some things which used to bother your conscience that don't anymore, and oughtn't to. There are some things which bother your conscience now, which never did before. And, of course, there are some things which have always been a matter of conscience with you, and always will be.

I started out in the ministry as a most earnest young man. There was a time when my conscience hurt if anything was laid on top of my Bible. And I didn't dare mark in it, so great was my respect. I couldn't stand for anyone's making jokes about the church or baptism or preaching—everything had to be strictly serious or God would be displeased. I remember sitting with my brothers in the college ministerial association and voting fiery resolutions against the evils of dancing on campus. Sure, we were earnest about that, but my mind's changed now. Back then, just looking at a girl in a bathing suit took on the proportions of fighting the devil himself. For awhile, in small rural churches, my conscience even bothered me about planning sermons in advance, because I had some feeling that you were just supposed to get up and speak from inspiration. Those thoughts don't trouble me anymore. But in their place, other concerns have grown—concerns I scarcely thought about then.

I have more conscience for the plight of minorities than when I preached my first sermon as a high-school boy in a small Southern town. My conscience increasingly questions the validity of war and violence. I'm not ready to say we shouldn't defend our lives and property, but I am no longer willing to see our country wage wars of international politics, and be personally silent. I have a conscience about that now.

I have a conscience about the ethics of evangelism which I never thought about before. Tactics of coercion and deceit aren't worthy of the God who speaks so much of truth and light. Even when the pressure begins to mount for more additions to the church membership, there are approaches which conscience won't let me use to try to get it done.

I have a conscience about protecting the environment which I never dreamed of when we thought our resources would last forever. And I believe I'm more conscious of the church serving the needs of people than I once was. The main idea before was how to get them to serve the church.

So much of it changes, don't you see? It's not that you forget your principles, it's just that you outgrow some and replace them with others. Your satisfaction is that you tried to be true to them while they were yours, and that some have stayed with you all the way.

If you will make the effort to study your own conscience, I'm sure you'll find the same pattern of change and learning, mixed with some consistency. The quest is the thing—the search for truth, the pursuit of integrity. We mustn't be ashamed of those changes. It's much more important to find truth than to preserve consistency. Paul's life was a tangled jungle of inconsistency, but he had this witness, that he had lived it in all good conscience, each step of the way. (See Acts 23:1.)

Conscience must learn from the mistakes of the past, but it mustn't spend a lifetime hurting over them. It mustn't drive us to despair. A conscience which batters a man day and night is an enemy, not a friend.

Conscience must cause us to be serious about life, yet not too serious—sure enough, but not too sure; clear in our estimate of others' views, but not intolerant; rewarded for our virtue, but not complacent or smug.

Conscience is no infallible guide. It may on occasion be perverted, misled, prostituted, and worse than valueless. At its best, it is man's struggle for self-awareness, self-evaluation, self-improvement, self-fulfillment, and moral sensitivity.

Conscience must be instructed by the Holy Spirit, and submissive to the lordship of Christ. Without this, the admonition "let your conscience be your guide" is the toss of a coin by a blind umpire.

Conscience must deal with the reasoning of the mind, not just the feelings of the emotions.

Conscience can bless you when all other blessings fail, when no one in all this whole earth understands, and that is its greatest victory.

Conscience has this as its great proof of validity, that it will sometimes lead a rational man to act against his own self-interest. You have heard it said of old: "George Washington chopped down a cherry tree; when his father said, 'Who did it?' George Washington said, 'Me.'" When a man does that; when he goes against the safe way out; when he quits his candidacy like Charles Weltner, whose conscience wouldn't support the democratic candidate in his state; when he loses his church because as pastor he refused to nod to a racist policy—then conscience has its finest hour.

Conscience will make a man useful to those who trust him, as they struggle to make their own decisions. My own "man for all seasons" pastored a church nearby. His conscience for the ethics of the ministry was so ruthless that I used him more than once to help me find peace.

Finally, let me share a few closing suggestions about your own quest for a good conscience. First, *we must educate our conscience in the issues of the day*. Conscience will not see what you don't *teach* it to see, or hear what you don't teach it to hear.

During my years of college and seminary education, there were times when the baby cried out for sleepy attention in the middle of the night. But I would seldom hear it. Other ears were programmed to that. Gerry always took care of it. But when the alarm clock chimed at 4:00 A.M. to begin my seventy-mile journey to an eight o'clock class, Gerry slept right on with a peaceful smile.

Now a person can't answer all the world's chimes and bells and cries of responsibility. No man's conscience is that strong. What we must do is give it a chance to see the needs about us, hear the appeals and arguments, and see where our efforts fit in the scheme of things.

A second suggestion is this: *We must overcome the tendency of the possible good to be the victim of the impossible best.* Almost anything a mortal man does is a compromise. A conscience which says, "Don't do anything unless it's your best," is going to strangle you. The miserable people who buy that philosophy are afraid to do anything, because they know it won't be perfect. We must realize our limitations and know that it's better to strive imperfectly, but conscientiously, than to sit around dreaming ways of perfection which we never even attempt. We're not going to save the whole world singlehanded. Conscience must allow us to break up the task into chunks of modest size, chunks we can handle. That isn't God's voice telling us we have to do it all, do the impossible, do it to perfection. That voice will lead man to discouragement and frustration and away from God.

The final word is this: *Let us honestly seek the truth of God, and then have faith to act with courage and boldness.*

A good conscience and an honest effort go hand in hand. The pastor of a struggling country church was asked by his official board to try to raise money from a large church in the city. Before he left, he gathered those men and asked if they could say in all good conscience that they had done everything possible within their own resources. He knew they hadn't, you see. And when they thought on it, they knew it too, and they raised all they needed.

What I'm stressing here is that our conscience must not be allowed to keep us in perpetual contemplation. The "paralysis of analysis" is a very real threat to Christian action. There are times when further discussion and consideration serve no purpose whatever, except to prolong a state of hesitation and uninvolvement. On such occasions, a conscience which keeps a red light flashing—"Heavens, don't decide or try to do anything, because you're still not sure if this is absolutely right"—that conscience becomes more of an excuse than a reason.

"There is a point at which everything becomes simple," wrote Dag Hammarskjold, "and there is no longer any question of choice, because all you have staked will be lost if you look back. Life's point of no return." [9]

Perhaps a normal lifetime passes many such points of deciding crucial issues. "Normal" certainly means also that we will look back at some of them across the years and wish for the chance of choosing all over again. We can't have that, of course. And a person can't be very involved in the moral struggles of life and achieve any consistent record of being always sure, much less always right. Our hope of consistency lies in this: that we strive always to be open in our motives, honest in our dealings, and true to whatever light we profess to follow.

Of a mortal man, this is all that God can possibly require. And it is no small task.

# Part V

## Integrity as Personal Wholeness

Dear Heavenly Father (If I may bother you just one more time):

I'd hoped, by now, that I could have arrived at some kind of decision about my life, and what you want from me. I'd hoped to get my problems all out of the way and just relax for a change. But it hasn't worked out that way, as you well know. And I want to apologize for the fact that I keep taking so much of your time and attention.

Where I am right now is just this—I'm in the process of becoming more the kind of person I think you'd want. The process seems awfully slow at times, and it certainly isn't easy. But when I look back at where I came from, I know the direction is good, even if the speed isn't.

I want to thank you, Sir, for all the help you've given me so far. And I really feel that one day soon your efforts will be rewarded. Can you be patient with me just a little longer?

# 13

## Those Hidden Feelings

From the time of the prophets on, the peoples of Israel and Judah had the misfortune of being a military and political buffer zone. Egypt, to the southwest, and the kingdoms of Mesopotamia, to the northeast, took turns trading this territory between them. The earlier period belonged more often to powerful Egypt, but in the eighth century B.C., a mighty king of Assyria became the power to reckon with. He captured a number of weaker tribes, and his conquest continued until great numbers of people were taken into exile, far from their homeland. In 587 B.C. Jerusalem fell; their Temple was destroyed; and many new faces joined their brothers in a bitter exile.

The place of their deportation was Babylon, and their prophets there were Ezekiel and Second Isaiah. The few who remained at home were hounded by their local enemies, the Edomites. After murdering their imposed governor, a number of them fled to Egypt for safety, including another prophet named Jeremiah.

The misery of those days continued until a new leader arose in the East—Cyrus, king of Persia. Isaiah called him "the Lord's anointed." In 538 B.C. Cyrus came to power and passed an edict allowing Israelites to return to their land. In 515 B.C. those who returned completed a rebuilding of their Temple in Jerusalem, and thus the period known as the Exile came to a close.

The trauma of the Exile was something like the cross in the New Testament. It was a sad, dark hour which was never to be forgotten. It was a time of loneliness, a time of suffering, a time of judgment, a time when those words from the cross would seem equally appropriate: "My God, my God, why hast thou forsaken me?"

Psalm 137 was written sometime during the exile. With powerful intensity, it expresses all the range of bitter feelings which trouble the heart in extreme circumstances. And although it's now something over 2,500 years old, it still has a profound and timely message. It's a people's lament; it's a pouring out of hidden feelings. It has the tone of a spirit which is tired but not crushed, a faith which is burdened but not extinguished, and a certain waiting for some kind of deliverance, which is still nowhere in sight. Here is what it said:

*By the waters of Babylon, there we sat down and wept, when we remembered Zion./ On the willows there we hung up our lyres./ For there our captors required of us songs, / and our tormentors, mirth, saying,/ "Sing us one of the songs of Zion!"*

*How shall we sing the Lord's song in a foreign land!/ If I forget you, O Jerusalem, let my right hand wither!/ Let my tongue cleave to the roof of my mouth, if I do not remember you,/ if I do not set Jerusalem above my highest joy!*

*Remember, O Lord, against the Edomites the day of Jerusalem,/ how they said, "Rase it, rase it! Down to its foundations!" / O daughter of Babylon, you devastator!/ Happy shall he be who requites you with what you have done to us!/ Happy shall he be who takes your little ones and dashes them against the rock! (Ps. 137).*

The greatest value of that lament is its ruthlessly honest expression of basic human feelings. Not all of those feelings are nice or pretty; some of them even sound irreligious and unchristian. They almost make us want to put a finger to our lips and use a scolding tone: "Don't say that, for goodness sake!" But how often do our polite smiles cover up the same feelings? And wouldn't it be better if we could know them like this, take them before God, and talk about them?

116

As an endeavor toward our own personal wholeness, let's consider four of the human feelings we find in this exilic lament. And as we do, let's try to see if they are really strangers to any of us.

The first is *the sorrow of a vanished past*—the loneliness of people homesick for what used to be (v. 1,5–6). They said: "We sat down and wept when we remembered Zion." *We had it, and now we've lost it,* they were saying. *Will we ever get it back?* Isn't there some of that in all of us?—that sorrow over something gone? And can't you feel it tugging at you when they say, *we wept when we remembered?*

We remember small towns where every face was familiar, where days were lazy and restful, where a "civil disturbance" was someone's dog barking at night, and teenage crime was two boys turning over an outhouse on Halloween.

We remember the loving securities of home, and long hours of child's play and fantasy, catching a fish for the first time, buying candy in a store, being young with years and years ahead, that are almost all used up now.

We remember the magic and mystery and excitement of that boy or girl we went out with—the first stirrings of what we then called "love," because the songs all told us to. Even our transgressions seemed sweet back then, and we think of that if we find now that what's left of it is just a ritual, an obligation, or a bargaining point.

Birds hatching in a nest; a night sky filled with the millions of stars you never see any more; your first high heels; all your old buddies in basic training camp; that first little apartment where you washed so many, many diapers; a mother or a father who's left you now—all of us have something back there, something of value, some hill of Zion, something to weep for when we know its gone and all we'll ever be able to do is remember.

And when we gather around us all that old furniture, old pictures, old cars, old books and Bibles, old knives and watches, old comic books, old records of corny radio programs—we're acting out this sorrow of a vanished past.

And of course the youth get restless with that, because it's ours, not theirs. It's an adult's way of saying: "Look here, young people, see how it was when I was young? Don't you wish you had it as good as this?" And that's why adults are so everlastingly curious about where the kids are going, and what they're doing, and what they're taking now; because it would only add to our sorrow if we thought they'd discovered something we missed! And part of the misery is that we'll never really know for sure whether they did or not.

The first feeling is sorrow, but the second one is shame—*the shame of a desperate plight* (vv. 2–3). The exiles are given no privacy. Wishing to be alone and do their work, they are forced into mockery. "Sing us one of your Zion songs," the captors say. And it gets so bad that when they hear the adversary coming, they hang up their harps on the willows in a rather tame sort of protest gesture.

Can you imagine those proud sons of Jacob being forced to sing their sacred songs for these invaders? What if they had to sing one like Psalm 46? *There is a river whose streams make glad the city of God,/the holy habitation of the Most High./God is in the midst of her, she shall not be moved;/God will help her right early./The nations rage, the kingdoms totter; he utters his voice, the earth melts. The Lord of hosts is with us; the God of Jacob is our refuge* (Ps. 46:4–7). That song always sounded good back in Jerusalem. Now here they were, almost overcome by the shame of their desperate plight, and God's seeming absence from giving them any help, and it was different singing it now.

But do you know, although they refused to sing the song, *they vowed to remember what the song was about?* They said: "If I forget you, O Jerusalem, let my right hand wither." You don't always have to sing the songs of Zion to carry some feeling about Zion in your heart. And in this there may be hope for some of our sons and daughters, who've upset us because they won't sing the song anymore. We can't make them sing it, and we shouldn't try to. But there is hope that though they refuse to sing the song, someday they'll remember what the song was about.

Israel's story was that in an alien land they began to cherish faith—the same faith which the prophets had often rebuked them for forsaking in their own land, in times of ease.

What if we could learn to serve God today as if we might not have the opportunity tomorrow? What if we would support the churches as if our utmost effort were required for their very survival? What if we took our citizenship as seriously in peacetime as we did when the shores were threatened by foreign invasion? Why do we take for granted the things that matter most, when there's no pressure on us? When times are good and we have every opportunity to sing the song of Zion, we couldn't care less. Only when we lose the chance do we begin to miss it—only when the shame of a desperate plight closes in around us.

Two of the issues of Teddy Roosevelt's second campaign were the Panama Canal and an uprising in Morocco. A movie called *The Wind and the Lion* was filmed about that period sometime ago. At one point in the film, a bright young American diplomat is telling his backward constituents about America's new inventions. He states it just like it was believed back then. "We have people," he said, "who can do things you can't begin to imagine. We have people who can do *anything!*" And that's what we thought. Any problem can be solved, we thought! Now, suddenly, we've come across some that don't seem to budge. And we who planned to live like kings over our problems, now feel more like captives to them. And it's hard to sing when it gets like that.

This brings us to a third feeling—*the misery of an empty worship* (v. 4). "How shall we sing the Lord's song in a foreign land?" Now I think they *should* have been able to sing in a foreign land, but I understand the misery there. Outward circumstances *shouldn't* matter to our worship, but sometimes they do. Some folks in a small Kentucky church just couldn't worship if the pastor didn't get on his knees when he led in prayer. People in all congregations get thrown out of gear if the music isn't just to their liking. Some wouldn't come at all if they knew the air conditioning wasn't going to work. And a lot of moderns can't sing the Lord's song for watching the time, or writing little notes to fellow pew-sitters, or thinking about dinner in just a little while now.

So how can we blame a defeated group of captives—carried away to a strange and savage land; separated from their temple and all their heritage; mocked and made fun of—saying "how can we sing the Lord's song *here*?"

Not every place and hour and frame of mind is suitable for giving praise to God. If you come to your church after a terrible family fight, which still isn't reconciled and likely will be taken up again as soon as you get home, you won't sing the Lord's song very well either!

A few times in my ministry, I've had to walk up to some pulpit and try to preach when I didn't feel at all like it. I'd heard some terribly unpleasant words from a member just a little while before. They stayed between me and everything I planned to say that morning. So I knew the misery of an empty worship. And if you've come very often to seek the Lord with all your heart, you know it too.

There's one other expressed feeling in this psalm which I think we ought to look at. It's *the anger of a troubled spirit* (vv. 7–9). The exiles curse the Edomites, their hostile neighbors, who rejoiced over them when Jerusalem fell. "Remember, O Lord, against the Edomites," they say. "Bring the same thing on them!" "Blessings on those who give them their due!" And then there's that terrible line about dashing their little children against the rocks.

It's possible that this language is all the stronger because, for them, any kind of action against the Edomites was impossible.

We curse the loudest, you see, when the words are all we have—as if we could win with them what we can't win, or won't try to win, any other way.

Something else is very curious about this invective. The Edomites were far away—miles and miles away to the southwest. The Babylonians were the people who really should have been cursed. But they were *too close*. They had ears that could hear, and swords that could cut, and whips that could punish. So curse the Edomites, way back home; they can't hear us!

That's the way anger does. It doesn't always work out in the open. It hides and waits and broods and plots. A man will take the anger he feels toward his wife—which he can't or won't express to her—and vent it on those who work with him. A woman will bring home the anger she feels over some social snub, and take it out on her children. Anger sneaks around, you see. And when a people suffers shame, as those Israelites did by the waters of Babylon, the question really isn't "how shall I take this?" The question is: "How shall I express the anger I feel, without bringing misery to myself and everyone around me, including those I love?" And right there the gospel says that God can help us.

The sorrow of a vanished past, the shame of a desperate plight, the misery of an empty worship, the anger of a troubled spirit—whatever the exile that brings those tormentors to our minds and hearts, our God will help us if we ask him. For he says to us, in all our strivings: "Come to me, all who labor and are heavy laden, and I will give you *rest*" (Matt. 11:28).

# 14

## On Weakness and Strength

A recent magazine article discussed a popular lady tennis star. In spite of her excellent record of winning matches, the article worried over some qualities which it described as weaknesses. She lacks what was called the "jugular instinct." She is even seen to smile upon losing a point. And heresy of heresies, she has been quoted as saying that "winning isn't everything." Then she has recently taken a husband, against her tennis manager's best judgment—all of this supposedly a sign of weakness.

A recent news broadcast reported on a bank president who delivers newspapers on a route in his neighborhood. A lot of folks think it's funny, but he's been doing it for two years now. And another story tells about a college Ph.D. who does laboring jobs in the summer and finds it fascinating. His most recent job was garbage collecting. In an interview he tells how a woman stood watching him from the back porch as he emptied her garbage into his sack, then asked him, as he shouldered it to leave: "Do you think you'll ever amount to anything?" The Ph.D. walked away laughing.

Those stories have some interesting implications for an inquiry into the meaning of weakness and strength. You see, the script we've all been handed doesn't allow for an athlete to be considerate, or for a bank president to be his neighbor's paperboy, or for a college professor to ride a garbage truck. Those are signs of weakness, not in keeping with what our society considers as worthy achievement.

The script says that strength is controlling others so that they are made to do your will with the least personal effort. Weakness is respecting the will and freedoms of others, and choosing a democratic style of leadership instead.

Strength is avenging yourself of every hostile act—not taking any mistreatment without returning it. Weakness is absorbing abuse while mentioning things like love and reconciliation. It's true the Bible tells us to leave vengeance to God, but most people believe a strong person ought to take care of it for himself—all the cowboy movies taught us that!

Strength is regarded as being able to act in your own best interest, without worrying about principles, laws, or the feelings or rights of others. And by this definition, weakness is expressed when a man subordinates his personal interest to a regard for such principles, laws, or feelings.

Strength means promoting your personal reputation at every possible opportunity; weakness shows in uplifting others at the expense of your own ambitions.

Strength means refusing to continue any human relationship in which the personal gain is less than the effort expended. It's weakness to have the kind of love which would "lay down his life for a friend."

To be strong means associating solely with those who can be of value to your own ambitions. Weakness is relating to others with a respect for *their* personal worth—not regarding their worth *to you*. Paul advised us to "Not be haughty, but associate with the lowly" (Rom. 12:16). But by the prevailing standards of our day, that's the counsel of weakness. A strong person always plays the game another way.

Strength is helping others only when it serves your own self-interest, and it's weakness to go around giving time and money without getting something back.

Have I confused you? Do you see the problem? It's just not easy to define what is strong and what is weak. In fact, as I searched for what the Bible teaches on this subject, I found at least four points of view.

First of all, the Bible has a view that *strength is strength*. The chronicles of the Old Testament abound with an admiration of power and might. The writer of Proverbs declares that "the glory of young men is their strength" (Prov. 20:29), and Isaiah's famous passage promises that in waiting on the Lord we shall renew our strength, mounting up with wings like eagles, running and not being weary (Isa. 40:31). One of Paul's great prayers in Ephesians is that we may be "strengthened with might through his Spirit in the inner man" and so "have power" (Eph. 3:16,18). And in his letter to the Colossians, he put it this way: "May you be strengthened with all power, according to his glorious might, for all endurance and patience with joy, giving thanks to the Father, who has qualified us to share in the inheritance of the saints of light" (Col. 1:11–12). It's interesting that Paul's Greek word for power was *dunamis,* from which we derive our word *dynamite.* So there is a sense in which the Bible offers dynamite-like power, instructs men in its use, and glories in the energy which is unleashed. This is the view that strength is strength.

In the second place, the Bible also has a viewpoint that *strength is weakness.* God confounds the mighty and exalts those of low degree (Luke 1:52). Let him who thinks he is standing in his strength take heed, lest he fall (1 Cor. 10:12). As Job saw so clearly, God doesn't share very much of his strength with the mighty: "With him are strength and wisdom; the deceived and the deceiver are his./He leads counselors away stripped, and judges he makes fools./He looses the bonds of kings, and binds a waistcloth on their loins./He leads priests away stripped, and overthrows the mighty./He deprives of speech those who are trusted, and takes away the discernment of the elders./He pours contempt on princes, and looses the belt of the strong" (Job 12:16–21).

Ezekiel and many of the other exilic prophets looked at

strength that way. Egypt was strong and mighty, but Ezekiel declared that "her proud might shall come to an end." Pharaoh's strong arm shall be broken, and God will scatter the Egyptians among the nations (see Ezek. 30).

Senator Sam Ervin made a somewhat similar observation about the men of the Nixon White House. He said that they were not seduced by money but by power, and that they resorted to evil means to promote what they thought to be good ends. Ervin stated that in the process they repudiated a Constitution which teaches a government of laws and not of men, and that ironically the lust for power was the weakness through which power was lost.[1] And I have the feeling that an Ezekiel or an Isaiah or a Jeremiah might have seen it that way, might have seen strength as weakness.

The Bible also has a view that *weakness is weakness*. Paul gives much space in his Roman letter to the problems of those who are "weak in the faith." [2] He wants his readers to bear with the failings of the weak. He counsels patience and understanding. Still it's clear that he looks on their weakness as weakness. It's certainly not a condition he recommends. And so let us turn to the last remaining option.

It is also possible to conclude that *weakness is strength*. To the Corinthians Paul wrote that "God chose what is foolish in the world to shame the wise, God *chose what is weak in the world to shame the strong*, God chose what is low and despised in the world, even things that are not, to bring to nothing things that are, so that no human being might boast in the presence of God" (1 Cor. 1:27–29). To illustrate how he understood the meaning of this in his own life, Paul continued by saying: "I decided to know nothing among you except Jesus Christ and him crucified. *And I was with you in weakness* and in much fear and trembling; and my speech and my message were not in plausible words of wisdom, but in demonstration of the Spirit and power, that your faith might not rest in the wisdom of men but in the power of

God" (1 Cor. 2:2–5). Later on, Paul returns to this discussion, saying: "I will all the more gladly boast of my weaknesses, that the power of Christ may rest upon me." And then he adds: *For when I am weak, then I am strong!* (2 Cor. 12:9–10). Isn't all of this discussion proposing the astonishing idea that weakness is strength?

To be strong means fortifying the "I" to most people. But that may leave a person isolated from others, and in that isolation he becomes lonely and afraid. His search for strength is counter-productive. Strengthening becomes weakening; the effort of fortifying his position leaves him more vulnerable than before. It's like holding your breath, which certainly doesn't work for long. To keep life going, you have to lose what you have and risk filling your lungs with a new supply.

What we're dealing with here is insecurity, and there are two kinds of it. There is destructive insecurity, and there is creative insecurity.

*Destructive insecurity* is where a person becomes afraid of everything, where he is paralyzed in his relationships with others and defensive in all his responses. Destructive insecurity makes a person self-regarding, self-protecting, suspicious, hypocritical, nervous, and without joy or love. Such a person is trying desperately to be secure, to be strong and not weak, but the cure only feeds the illness. That kind of weakness is truly weakness, and no one ought to recommend or encourage it.

But there is another kind of insecurity, *a creative insecurity*, a growth-stimulating, strength-producing insecurity. Instead of becoming frantic to fortify and defend itself, this kind of insecurity is able to live with vulnerability and exposure. Wasn't this the way of Christ? Did he ever do anything at all to make himself secure against harm or hurt? The one time anyone ever tried to defend him with a sword, he rebuked the man. Because he was a person with no defenses to secure and maintain, he was in a position to take the risk of helping others, and the risk of saying

126

what he believed. *His strength was his weakness, and his weakness was his strength.*

You see, the more we are vulnerable to pain, the greater will be our possibility of joy. But the more we fortify ourselves against the possibility of pain, the less will be our possibility of that joy. Remember how the book of Hebrews said that Jesus endured the cross *"for the joy that was set before him"* (Heb. 12:2)? When you rid yourself of the possibility of pain, you rid yourself also of the possibility of joy. It's like a sensitive boy who gets hurt, and reacts by withdrawing into himself to be the school's "tough guy." It's like a young lady, hurt in love, who closes off the possibility of future pain by putting up a big high fence around her heart.

The great American family rerun is the story of a poor boy who works his way up from nothing. He finally succeeds in giving his children all the security he lacked. But they suffocate because of *too much* ease, and the boredom that goes with it, and one day they throw it all away in search of the excitement of the same insecurity from which he sought to protect them.

It's interesting to ponder Thomas Harris' four "life positions" in the light of this discussion of creative insecurity. Do you remember them? "I'm not OK, but you're not OK either"; "I'm not OK, but you're OK"; "I'm OK, and you're not OK"—and the last is the one he used as the title for his bestselling book: "I'm OK, You're OK." Reflecting on the biblical view of weakness and strength, I would suggest another possible stance—one which reflects an appreciation for some measure of creative insecurity. It would be this: *I'm almost OK—but not quite!*

W. Hale White, a biographer of John Bunyan, reflected that principle to his study when he wrote: "We may say of men like Bunyan that it is not their strength taken by itself which makes them remarkable and precious, but rather the conflict of strength and weakness." [3]

Have you ever noticed how the Bible keeps telling us to do things associated with weakness? *Confess your faults* one to

127

another, it says. Isn't that weakness? You could really hurt your reputation and give your enemy advantage by doing that!

It says to *admit your limitations,* that you know in part and preach in part. You can't be known as an expert and do much admitting like that. If you're not sure, just throw out some technical stuff and leave a cold trail behind you!

We're told to *forgive others their trespasses.* Wouldn't we be stronger by keeping them indebted to us? Certainly we would! This is clearly a counsel of weakness.

Other examples of it are almost endless: *Be a servant of others,* washing their dirty feet. When someone compels you to go a mile by law, *go the second mile* on your own. *Be willing to suffer* persecution without taking vengeance.

In fact, the thing that strikes you so often as you read the gospel is how utterly *impractical* it is—how unworkable, uninviting, and unthinkable. Paul called it a "scandal," you know. And yet, as you consider those who have followed it, and compare them with those who haven't, you begin to wonder if everything isn't somehow turned around. Maybe the practical is really the impractical; maybe protection is really throwing it away; maybe vulnerability is really a strength; maybe the winners are really the losers; maybe those who inherit the earth are to be the meek after all.

To the mind of secular man, the cross must seem a pitiful symbol of weakness. Even at the time, who could have looked upon it and imagined any further strength for this man and his frail cause? Why, the man who carried the cross had fallen under its load. The only property he left behind was the coat off his back, and they took that away and gambled for it. And the only disciples he could muster in that dark hour were a handful of crying women. Weakness? . . . strength? . . . what kind of evaluation can be given to such an inconclusive, unimpressive event?

Strange as it may appear, here is the best statement of it ever given: "He has shown strength with his arm,/he has scattered the proud in the imagination of their hearts,/he has put down the mighty from their thrones,/and exalted those of low degree," (Luke 1:51–52).

*Weakness has won out, don't you see? The kingdoms of the world have become the kingdom of our Lord and of his Christ, and he shall reign for ever and ever.* (See Rev. 11:15.)

# 15

## On Taking Too Much for Granted

"Every one who comes to me and hears my words and does them, I will show you what he is like: he is like a man building a house, who dug deep, and laid the foundation upon rock; and when a flood arose, the stream broke against that house, and could not shake it, because it had been well built. But he who hears and does not do them is like a man who built a house on the ground without a foundation; against which the stream broke, and immediately it fell, and the ruin of that house was great" (Matt. 7:24–27, author's translation).

*There it stands—the house I built. It still looks pretty good, if you look at it from over here. From here you can't see those terrible cracks, and the wall leaning over, and the many-gabled roof, ready to come falling in.*

*It's funny—some days when I look at it, I see nothing but this awful fracturing. Things I thought to be so strong, breaking in two; things I thought would last a lifetime or longer, floating away to who-knows-where; things I spent so very much time on, gone in a minute—this is what I see. And on those days, I have to fight a dreadful gloom of knowing that before long now, nothing will be left of all I've built.*

*For awhile there, it was sheer ecstasy—my housebuilding. I was charmed with my dreams; I was busy in my work; I saw the house becoming day by day. Now I recall that in those days some people asked me questions which I brushed aside—questions about the soundness of my plans; questions about footings, and water flowing when the hard rains fell; questions which seemed irrelevant to the progress I planned for that day; questions I didn't have time for.*

*It still looks pretty good, if you stand over here. Sometimes I can still close my eyes and see it just like I planned for it to be: large and strong and full of rooms to house the memorabilia of my success. I planned for doors which would open wide to receive the crowds who'd come to stare and wonder in jealous admiration— the men I had bettered in the competition of business; and their wives, who would use my obvious achievements, to chide the laziness of their husbands.*

*There it stands—the house I built. "Standing" is the word I use, but falling is the right one. My money is spent, my strength is gone; my time is all used up, and my house is falling down before my very eyes.*

*Let me tell you about the sand—that wretched, miserable sand, with all its blowing, washing, shifting, settling instability. I never thought about it when I rushed at starting my house, all so eager. The wind, the rain—I never knew, amid those peaceful days of building, the force, the punishment, the battering stress of rushing air and water, and the pitifully weak resistance of the sand.*

*What I built was strong, I thought. Hadn't I done it well? I took for granted that the worth of things I handled was all that mattered. But there's more. After the fall, the wreckage tells that you have to build on something—a contact, a trust, a joining with some other. The integrity of your structure is not just that it's good in itself, but that it has achieved a vital dependence. That may have been the only thing I lacked, and my misery is that I took it for granted.*

*They say my house is worthless now. All my money, all my time, all my toil, sweat, pain, and grief—worthless. And the dreams I had for my house are washed away with those muddy waters that come rushing down. Now they tell people to stay away. "Unsafe . . . Condemned," they say. And the jealous*

131

*admirers I had hoped to draw are laughing.*

*See that other house, standing over there? It's a good house, they say. And the soundness of that house is my pain, because it was my contemporary's. We built together, and I thought mine would be so much the better, for there were so many days he was doing little things, and I was building. He spent so much time in study and measurement and decidings, and diggings here and there. I was far ahead, because while he went around in all this seeming confusion, I was half-done already.*

*What on earth can I possibly do now? There it stands—the house I built. I can't live in it; I can't repair it; I can't sell it. Sooner or later, I'll grow tired of looking at the ruins and thinking how it might have been. Do you suppose it's too late to leave this sloppy mess and make a new start?*

This is an apt parable for multitudes of modern sand-builders. It illustrates the peril of taking too much for granted, of living at random, of living without awareness. It stands in judgment on all our structures of foolishness, all our pragmatic preoccupations, and all our tendencies for tall building, based on shallow digging. And it seems an appropriate symbol of some badly needed reappraisals in our personal and national life.

Haven't we Americans, for some years now, been hoping to build a great house for the whole world to marvel at? And we've been so busy at it, so charmed with our dreams, that we never noticed it all rested on the sands of greed and pride and dishonesty and secularism. And then the weather changed on us. Winds blew; floods came and beat upon our house. National disgrace, national scandal, national defeat, national shortages, national disunity—suddenly we're left with a lot of unpaid bills, a lot of shattered dreams, a lot of mess we can't seem to clean up, and a lot of neighbors looking at us and laughing. And now we're in the situation of asking what on earth we can possibly do to reestablish ourselves on something solid.

In a situation like that, you need to look farther down the road than just to the next gas stop. You need to ask where the road goes, and what business you have going there. A little girl raised that question one time. Her family had left home in a hurry, and failed to inform her of their destination. Her questions of "where are we going" were put off in favor of some quick stops and more urgent discussion. Only after several miles did she get an opportunity to put her question in a somewhat altered form: "Daddy, when we get where we're going, where will we be?"

*When I get this house built, what's it going to be like?*

*When we get this factory constructed—making this product, employing these people, discharging these wastes—is it going to help us or hurt us?*

*When I get this education, what am I going to do with it?*

*When we've lived together for thirty years, will we still love one another?*

*When my children have grown up to follow the value system they've learned from me, what will they be like?*

*When I've reached the top of the last hill I see, will there be anywhere left to go?*

*If a man die, shall he live again?*

In situations like those, when the footing underneath feels slippery instead of solid, a man tends to look for something basic that he might have missed. It's a familiar situation for a football coach. Things have been going along well—games won easily—then all at once comes an unexpected defeat. You don't turn to your fancy stuff in situations like that. You go back and work on the fundamentals: how to make tackles, execute blocks, catch passes—basic stuff like that. Someone says a good team takes those for granted. But that may just be the problem. You took too much for granted.

As members of churches, it's fun to sit around and argue the fine points of how the church should allocate its resources. And it's also fun to design fancy plays in the form of innovative programs. But the foundation for all that is the personal steward-

133

ship of the church's members—the dedication of dollars to the service of the Kingdom. And unless we execute that basic Christian task, all our planning is building on sand.

As Christian parents, it's certainly important to keep up on current affairs. But in the process, we ought not to take for granted the conversion of our own children, assuming that because *we* are Christians, *they* will be too. That's overlooking something very basic, and taking too much for granted.

As laymen of the church, it's good to read and discuss the latest theology. But how silly it is to see otherwise intelligent persons go chasing off after intricate and speculative theories, without a basic foundation in the teachings of the Bible, or the lessons of Christian history. The Sunday School hour may not always be the most exciting of the week, because it's digging. But woe to the person who rushes into the building of his life, without some kind of digging which secures its foundations.

There are many ways this sand-building takes its toll on us. We take it for granted that just exposing people to ethical teaching will result in their commitment to ethical conduct. But a house like that won't stand. We take it for granted that America is a Christian nation, that anyone who lives here has heard the gospel and can respond to it if he decides to. Missionary work is what the church does in foreign lands, not here. But that's taking far too much for granted, and building the future of the church on the sands of a meager effort.

On the most personal level, sand-building goes on when a man takes for granted that he can ever truly live without searching out the meaning of his existence. Someone once told me that I ask a lot of questions in my sermons. I realize some people don't like questions. They just want answers, put in neat little piles like food in a cafeteria. But as you consider those two houses in the story Jesus told, you must realize that *questions made the difference*. The wise builder had paused to ask where and upon what he should build. He had probed beneath the superficial; he had dug deep to secure his foundation.

That refusal to take life for granted is the basis of all religious conduct, and all personal integrity. The places where you need to get a shovel and begin to dig may not be the same as your neighbor's on the hill, but here are some possibilities.

*To keep from putting off too long the things you most want to do in life.*

*To find someone who will honestly listen to what you feel inside.*

*To gain the freedom to be the shout, and not the echo.*

*To find a faith that relates to today and to tomorrow, to the visible and to the invisible; for if in this life only we have hope, we are of all men most miserable.*

*To kneel in the presence of one to whom all praise truly belongs, who hasn't fooled us with cheap tricks, who isn't plastic, who is true and just and holy.*

*To bring a cup and drink of the Water of life, which, having drunk, a man will never thirst again.*

## NOTES—Part 1

[1] This reflective monologue, intended to set a context for the following discussion, was given from a separate place when this material was originally delivered as a sermon. I selected a spot well away from the pulpit to symbolize the difference in "roles." Although an intelligent congregation can pick up such role changes quite readily, some added emphasis (such as the change of speaking location) is helpful.

[2] Anthem "O Saviour of the World," Sir John Goss (Bryn Mawr, Pennsylvania: Theodore Presser Co.) Lyrics slightly abridged to eliminate repetitions.

[3] Frank S. Mead, *The Encyclopedia of Religious Quotations* (Old Tappan, New Jersey: Fleming H. Revell Company, 1965), p. 268.

[4] The "verbs of God's action" in this and the three preceding paragraphs were selected from actual quotations in the Old and New Testaments.

[5] I realize that the force of this reference to the Nixon Administration will become weaker as time passes. But for those who can still recall the "law and order" campaign speeches of Nixon and Agnew, it must surely still have meaning.

[6] Quoted by Reinhold Niebuhr. *The Nature and Destiny of Man*, Vol. 1 (New York: Charles Scribner's Sons, Scribner Library Edition, 1964), pp. 186–87.

[7] Quoted by Reinhold Niebuhr. *Ibid*, p. 189.

[8] Niebuhr, *ibid*, pp. 209–10.

[9] John Killinger, *For God's Sake, Be Human* (Waco: Word Books, 1970), p. 19.

[10] I have preserved here the language and feeling of the original presentation of this monologue to a Sunday congregation. Because of the harshness of the critic's words, he takes on the character of an intruder—a disturber of worship. The reader may gain something beneficial by imagining that setting.

## NOTES—Part II

[1] Reported by Baptist Press, February 1973.

[2] Howard Butt, *The Velvet Covered Brick* (New York: Harper & Row, 1973), p. 86.

[3] An illustration I first found in Charles Merrill Smith, *How to Become a Bishop Without Being Religious* (Garden City, N. Y.: Doubleday and Co., Inc., 1965), p. 3.

[4] The work by Smith already referred to contains a humorous though penetrating portrayal of ministerial hypocrisy.

[5] Jerald C. Brauer, ed., *The Westminster Dictionary of Church History* (Philadelphia: Westminster Press, 1971), pp. 459–60.

[6] William Neil, ed., *Concise Dictionary of Religious Quotations* (Grand Rapids: Eerdmans Publishing Company, 1974), pp. 89–90.

[7] *Ibid.*, p. 89.

[8] *Ibid.*, p. 126.

## NOTES—Part III

[1] Other than general reading and news reports, my primary sources for Watergate events mentioned here are two: Carl Bernstein and Bob Woodward, *All the President's Men* (New York: Warner Communications Company, Warner Paperback Library Edition, 1975); and Barry Sussman, *The Great Cover-up: Nixon and the Scandal of Watergate* (New York: The New American Library, Inc., Signet Edition, 1974).

[2] Henry Steele Commager, "Watergate and the Schools," *Today's Education* (September-October, 1974), p. 22.

[3] It was originally proposed that the title of this book should be "Watergate Isn't Very Far from Here." The publisher wisely judged that by the time of its appearance, public interest in articles about Watergate would be diminished greatly. I would simply ask the reader to question *what* we learned, *what* safeguards were established, *what* repentance took place, and *what* national decisions were reached other than to forget it as soon as possible.

[4] See, for example, an article by Merrill Sheils and William Schmidt, "The Cheaters," *Newsweek* (April 21, 1975), p. 97.

[5] Raven is quoted and his views summarized in an article by Robert J. Trotter, "Watergate: A Psychological Perspective," *Science News*, Vol. 106, p. 378.

[6] Mead, *op. cit.*, p. 313.

[7] *Ibid.*, p. 311.

## NOTES—Part IV

[1] Reinhold Niebuhr, *The Nature and Destiny of Man,* Vol. I (New York: Charles Scribner's Sons, Scribner Library Edition, 1964), p. 207.

[2] Frank S. Mead, ed., *The Encyclopedia of Religious Quotations* (Old Tappan, New Jersey: Fleming H. Revell Company, 1965), p. 117.

[3] *Ibid.*, p. 118.

[4] Kathryn Rogers Deering in *Ventures in Worship,* David James Randolph, ed. (Nashville: Parthenon Press, 1973), p. 88.

[5] Ralph L. Woods, ed., *The Modern Handbook of Humor* (New York: McGraw-Hill Book Company, 1967), p. 144.

[6] Mead, *op. cit.*, p. 117.

[7] *Ibid.*

[8] Quoted in an article "The Conscience of Leon Jaworski," *Esquire,* February, 1975, pp. 97, 150.

[9] Dag Hammarskjold, *Markings* (London: Faber and Faber, 1964), p. 70.

## NOTES—Part V

[1] I heard him say this in a speech to a seminar of the Christian Life Commission, Southern Baptist Convention, in Louisville, Kentucky in March, 1975.

[2] See especially chapter 14.

[3] W. Hale White, *John Bunyan* (New York: Charles Scribner's Sons, 1904), pp. 25–26.